Barbados Travel Guide 2023

"Discover the Tropical Paradise: Your Ultimate Guide to Barbados in 2023"

Jayden Gray

Copyright © 2023, Jayden Gray.

All rights reserved.

No part of this publication may be reproduced, distributed, or transmitted in any form or by any means, including photocopying, recording, or other electronic or mechanical methods, without the prior written permission of the publisher, except in the case of brief quotations embodied in critical reviews and certain other noncommercial uses permitted by copyright law.

Table of contents

I. INTRODUCTION
II. PLANNING YOUR TRIP
III. EXPLORING BRIDGETOWN
    Top Attractions in Bridgetown

    Shopping and Dining in Bridgetown

    Nightlife Bridgetown

IV. DISCOVERING BARBADOS BEACHES
    Top Beaches in Barbados

    Water Activities and Sports

    Beach Safety Tips

V. EXPLORING THE NATURAL BEAUTY OF BARBADOS
    National Parks and Reserves

    Hiking and Nature Trails

    Wildlife and Marine Life

    Botanical Gardens

VI. HISTORICAL AND CULTURAL SITES
    Historical Plantations and Museums

UNESCO World Heritage Sites

Cultural and Art Festivals

Local Cuisine and Culinary Experiences

VII. SPORTS AND RECREATION

Diving and Water Sports

Golfing in Barbados

Cricket and Other Sports

Wellness and Spa Retreats

VIII. ISLAND EXCURSIONS

IX. PRACTICAL INFORMATION

Money and Currency Issues

Health and Safety Tips

Communication and Internet

Useful Phrases and Local Etiquette

Navigating the Island

X. SHOPPING AND SOUVENIRS

XII. EVENTS AND FESTIVALS

XIII. BEYOND TOURISM

XIV. FINAL THOUGHTS AND TRAVEL TIPS

I. INTRODUCTION

Welcome to Barbados, a lush paradise tucked away in the Caribbean Sea's pristine seas. Barbados provides an exceptional vacation experience with its immaculate white sand beaches, colorful culture, and kind people. You will find all the information you want in our travel manual to ensure that your trip to this beautiful island in 2023 is as enjoyable as possible.

As the "Gem of the Caribbean," Barbados is a tiny island country in the Lesser Antilles. Barbados, which is well-known for its picturesque scenery, has a wide variety of attractions to suit the interests of any tourist.

Barbados has something for everyone, whether you want to unwind on sun-drenched beaches, explore historical monuments, indulge in water sports, or get to know the local culture. Barbados' topography is distinguished by its flat land and more than 60 kilometers of gorgeous coastline. The island is renowned for its beautiful beaches, where you can bask in the sun, swim in the clear seas, and engage in several water sports including sailing, snorkeling, and scuba diving. From the vibrant vibe of Mullins Beach to the peace of Crane Beach, which is famed for its powdery pink sand, each beach has its distinct appeal.

Beyond its beautiful beaches, Barbados is home to a lively culture and a long history that is visible throughout the island. The nation's capital, Bridgetown, is a bustling center of activity and a UNESCO World Heritage Site.

Visit St. Nicholas Abbey, a 17th-century plantation home, and the Garrison, a British military structure from the colonial period, among other historical sites in this area. An interesting look into the island's history may be found at the Barbados Museum and Historical Society.

Attend one of the various festivals and events that are held throughout the year to fully experience the local culture. Barbados' most well-known event, the Crop Over Festival, is a colorful carnival that marks the conclusion of the sugar cane harvest.

This event is an accurate reflection of the spirit and customs of the island, from the vibrant costumes and upbeat calypso music to the street parties and delectable Bajan food. Another highlight is the Oistins Fish Festival, where you may sample recently caught seafood and take in the colorful ambiance of this fishing community.

Barbados is a haven for those who like the great outdoors and the natural world. Visit the Andromeda Botanic Gardens, a refuge of rare plants and flowers, to discover the island's natural splendor, or go trekking in the lovely Welchman Hall Gully. Animal enthusiasts may learn about Barbados' distinctive fauna, which includes the Hawksbill turtles that lay their eggs along the island's beaches and the Green Monkey, the island's unofficial mascot.

In terms of useful information, this guide will provide you the crucial specifics on the ideal time to visit, visa needs, travel possibilities, and suggested lodging. If you want to explore the island at your speed, you may discover advice on getting about the island, utilizing the public transit system, and hiring a car.

This travel guide offers thorough information, expert advice, and recommended itineraries to improve your experience, whether you're visiting Barbados for the first time or returning after a long absence. Prepare to savor the lively culture, soak in the sunlight, and make lifelong memories on the alluring island of Barbados.

II. PLANNING YOUR TRIP

There are a few important things to think about while organizing your vacation to Barbados to guarantee a hassle-free and delightful experience. Careful preparation can help you make the most of your stay on the island, from choosing the ideal time to come to knowing visa requirements and booking travel and lodging. Here are some crucial suggestions to assist you in organizing your 2023 vacation to Barbados.

- ***Best Time to Visit***

Barbados' dry season, which lasts from December to April, is the ideal time to visit. The best weather is present at this time, with no rain, plenty of sunlight, and comfortable temperatures between the mid-70s and mid-80s F (20 to 30 C). There will be more people and more expensive accommodations during the dry season, which is also the busiest travel season.

The off-peak months of May through June and November might be a fantastic choice if you want a more sedate and affordable vacation. These times of year provide a good mix between pleasant weather and fewer visitors. Though there may be a few sprinkles here and there, the weather is still beautiful. The cost of lodging is often cheaper, and you'll have more space to take in the sights unhindered by crowds.

Due to the Atlantic hurricane season, the low season, which lasts from July to October, is marked by higher humidity and a greater likelihood of rainfall. If you're interested in attending cultural events, festivals, or diving, this time of year may not be the best for you to visit the beach and relax.

This period offers large savings on lodging and entertainment, making it a desirable choice for tourists on a tight budget. It's crucial to remember that Barbados has relatively warm weather year-round, with most rainfall coming in brief spurts. The island's infrastructure is well-developed and capable of coping with tropical weather.

The ideal time to go to Barbados ultimately depends on your priorities and interests. The dry season is your best choice if you value a lively environment and great beach weather. Think about traveling during the shoulder seasons if you want a more sedate and budget-friendly experience. Whenever you decide to go to Barbados, you will have a wonderful experience because of the island's friendly people, gorgeous beaches, and dynamic culture.

- *Visa Requirements*

Depending on your country of citizenship and the length of your stay, different visas are needed for Barbados. The basic information about obtaining a visa to visit Barbados is as follows:

- **Visa-Free Entry:** For stays up to 90 days, citizens of a large number of nations including the United States, Canada, the

United Kingdom, and the majority of the member states of the European Union do not need a visa to visit Barbados. This is true for trips for work, pleasure, and visiting friends and family. It's crucial to remember that the immigration officer has the last word on how long you may remain; based on their evaluation, it can be fewer than 90 days.

- **Electronic Travel Authorization (ETA):** Some nations, like Brazil, China, India, and Russia, demand their nationals get an ETA before visiting Barbados. You may get entry authorization into the nation by completing a quick online application known as the ETA. It is advised to apply for the ETA at least 72 hours before the day you plan to depart.

- **Visa-required National:** Nationals from some nations, such as Nigeria, Ghana, and other Middle Eastern nations, must get a visa before visiting Barbados, regardless of the reason for their trip or the length of their stay. If you have a passport from one of these nations, it's crucial to get in touch with the Barbadian embassy or consulate in your area well in advance to learn about the criteria and visa application procedure.

- **Extension of Stay:** To extend your stay over the time that was originally authorized, go to the immigration office in Bridgetown and submit an application. Extensions are not guaranteed, therefore it is best to schedule your visit during the originally allotted time frame.

Regardless of your nationality, it's crucial to make sure your passport is valid for at least six months after the day you want to leave Barbados.

Before visiting Barbados, it's important to confirm the most recent visa regulations that apply to your situation and nationality. The most precise and up-to-date information on visa requirements may be found on the official website of the Barbados Immigration Department or by contacting the closest Barbadian embassy or consulate.

It's important to keep in mind that visa restrictions might vary, so it's best to remain informed and make plans appropriately to guarantee a simple and trouble-free admission into Barbados.

- *Transportation Options*

Barbados has a range of means of transportation that may be used to move about the island and see its attractions. The primary modes of transportation are as follows:

1. Public Buses: Barbados's public bus system is a convenient and reasonably priced means to get across the island. According to their routes, the buses are color-coded, with blue buses being the most prevalent. Most places are covered by the bus network, including well-known tourist attractions. Bus routes have different frequencies of service, and they run from early in the morning to late at night.

2. Taxis: Taxis are a handy and pleasant means of transportation and are widely accessible in Barbados. Taxis that are officially recognized may be identified by their "Z" license plates. Before beginning your trip, it is recommended to haggle and agree on the fee since taxis sometimes do not use meters. Hotels, tourist hotspots, and authorized taxi stops are all places to find taxis.

3. Renting a Vehicle: Travelers who want more freedom and flexibility to explore the island at their speed sometimes choose to rent a vehicle. A variety of local and foreign automobile rental businesses provide customers with a selection of cars. Driving on the left side of the road is essential in Barbados, so be sure your license is up to date. You should be aware that Barbados has stringent traffic rules and speed restrictions, so you should get acquainted with them.

4. Scooters and Motorcycles: Renting a motorbike or scooter to navigate Barbados is another alternative. If you're comfortable riding a bike, it may be a pleasant and exciting way to explore the island. You'll need a driver's license that is currently valid, and you should observe local traffic regulations and safety procedures, just like when you hire a vehicle.

5. Ridesharing Services: In Barbados, you may use ridesharing services like Uber and Lyft. They provide a practical and often less expensive alternative to conventional taxis. However, it's crucial to confirm that the ridesharing service is available while you're visiting the island since availability varies.

6. Bicycle Rentals: You may hire bicycles in Barbados if you want a more environmentally friendly and physically active form of transportation. Bicycles are available for hire at a few places of lodging and other businesses on the island. Even though Barbados has some designated bike lanes, it is vital to remember that the roads may sometimes be congested and small.

It's crucial to take into account things like the distances you'll be going, the places you wish to see, and your chosen amount of freedom when organizing your transportation in Barbados. Each mode of transportation has benefits, so picking the one that best meets your requirements and interests will make your time spent visiting Barbados easier and more fun.

- *Accommodation Options*

Barbados has a wide variety of lodging choices to accommodate all tastes and price ranges. There are accommodations for everyone, including modest guesthouses, boutique hotels, and luxury resorts. Here are a few prominent lodging options in Barbados:

1. Luxury Resorts: Barbados is renowned for its top-tier resorts that are positioned along the breathtaking coastline. These resorts include opulent extras such as roomy suites or rooms, a variety of dining choices, spa services, swimming pools, and access to private beaches. They offer visitors a variety of activities and entertainment alternatives, as well as first-rate service.

2. Boutique Hotels: There are many wonderful boutique hotels in Barbados that provide a more individualized and private experience. These hotels often include distinctive architectural designs, uniquely furnished rooms, and an emphasis on individualized service. They could include extras like on-site dining options, spa services, and private gardens.

3. Guesthouses and Bed and Breakfasts: Opt for a guesthouse or bed and breakfast for a more genuine and cost-effective experience. These more intimate lodgings are owned by families and provide a warm and inviting ambiance. They provide cozy lodging, a hearty meal, and a chance to mingle with the people.

4. Vacation Rentals: There are many different types of vacation rentals in Barbados, from condominiums and flats to beachfront homes and villas. You may live independently, have a kitchen for self-catering, and experience local life when you rent a holiday home. Families or bigger parties might consider vacation rentals.

5. All-Inclusive Resorts: Barbados is home to some all-inclusive resorts that provide hassle-free vacations to visitors. These resorts often provide a single package that includes lodging, food, drinks, and some activities. They are a practical choice for people who would rather have everything handled centrally.

Consider aspects including location, accessibility to services and activities, desired experience type, and price range when selecting lodging in Barbados. It is essential to make reservations in advance to ensure your preferred option, particularly during busy travel times. Check the lodgings' ratings and reviews to make sure they live up to your expectations.

There are many different lodging alternatives available in Barbados, each with its special charm and conveniences. When visiting this beautiful Caribbean island, you're sure to discover the ideal lodging, whether you're looking for luxury and relaxation or a more genuine and affordable experience.

III. EXPLORING BRIDGETOWN

Welcome to Bridgetown, the vivacious and UNESCO-designated Barbados capital city. Bridgetown, which is situated on the island's southwest coast, is a thriving center of culture, history, and Caribbean beauty. Bridgetown provides tourists with a thrilling experience that highlights the distinctive character of Barbados with its rich past, colonial buildings, lively markets, and friendly residents.

History and Architecture: Bridgetown was founded as a British colonial town in the 17th century, and since that time it has had a colorful history. The Careenage, a picturesque stream that still flows through the center of the city, was previously crossed by a native Amerindian bridge, from whence the city got its name. The architecture of the city is influenced by British colonization, including lovely examples of Georgian-style structures and important historical sites like the Parliament Buildings and St. Michael's Cathedral.

Historical Landmarks: Several noteworthy historical sites in the city provide a window into Barbados' history. The Garrison, a historic British military installation that was essential to the island's security, is one of the most recognizable locations. Many historically significant structures, like the George Washington House, where the first president of the United States once stayed, can be found in the Garrison neighborhood. The Barbados Museum and Historical Society, located in a former British military jail, is another noteworthy site. Visitors may look around the displays here to learn more about the island's history, culture, and natural heritage.

Shopping and Market: Bridgetown has a wide range of shopping alternatives to suit all likes and budgets, making it a shoppers' paradise. The primary shopping area of the city is Broad Street, which is lined with a variety of upscale shops, boutiques, and duty-free stores selling jewelry, clothing, and luxury items. Visit the vibrant Cheapside Market or the Pelican Craft Centre for a more regional and genuine shopping experience. Both places offer a large selection of handicrafts, regional artwork, and traditional Barbadian goods.

Culture and Cuisines: Bridgetown is a melting pot of ethnicities, which is reflected in its thriving artistic community and wide range of culinary options. Numerous art galleries in the city display the creations of local and regional artists. Regular cultural activities are held at the Barbados Museum, including art exhibits, talks, and performances. Bridgetown has a wide variety of eating establishments, from fine-dining establishments that specialize in international and fusion cuisine to street food vendors selling traditional Bajan delicacies. Don't pass up the chance to sample regional delicacies like cou-cou, flying fish, and macaroni pie.

Sandy Beaches and Waterfront: Bridgetown is endowed with gorgeous sandy beaches and a stunning coastline. Carlisle Bay is well-known for its clean seas and is a great location for swimming, snorkeling, and other water activities. The Careenage, a historic canal in the city, has riverfront pubs and restaurants where you can unwind and take in the scenery. It also provides picturesque boat cruises. Additionally accessible is the well-known Pebbles Beach, renowned for its serene seas and breathtaking sunsets.

The combination of history, culture, and scenic beauty in Bridgetown is mesmerizing. This dynamic city encourages you to enjoy the warm warmth and charm of Barbados, whether you're seeing its historical monuments, buying trinkets, or just taking in the lively environment.

Top Attractions in Bridgetown

Barbados' capital city, Bridgetown, is home to many sites that highlight the island's extensive history, thriving culture, and stunning natural surroundings. Some of Bridgetown's top attractions, which range from breathtaking beaches to historic sites, are listed below:

1. Parliament Buildings: The Parliament Buildings, which are a well-known landmark and a reminder of the island's colonial heritage, are situated in the center of Bridgetown. The Parliament of Barbados is housed in the neo-Gothic building, which is a representation of the democracy practiced on the island. Visitors may stroll around the surrounding gardens and take in the architectural splendor of the buildings.

2. Historic Bridgetown and its Garrison (UNESCO World Heritage Site): Bridgetown's whole historic city as well as the surrounding garrison region have been recognized by UNESCO as a World Heritage Site. Discover the colonial structures that have been maintained, such as the Barbados Museum and Historical Society, the Jewish Synagogue, and St. Michael's Cathedral. The region is historically significant and provides an intriguing window into Barbados' past.

3. Carlisle Bay: Carlisle Bay, a gorgeous beach known for its pristine waters and abundant marine life, is located not far from Bridgetown. The area has several shipwrecks to explore and good snorkeling and scuba diving possibilities. To appreciate the splendor of the bay, take a catamaran trip, relax on the sandy beaches, or engage in water sports.

4. Cheapside Market: Take in as much of the colorful local culture as you can there. With its brightly colored kiosks offering fresh food, spices, regional crafts, and souvenirs, this lively market provides a sensory treat. As you take in the genuine ambiance, try some traditional Bajan foods and chat with the welcoming merchants.

5. Barbados Museum and Historical Society: The Barbados Museum and Historical Society provides a thorough look at the island's history, culture, and natural resources. It is located in the old British military jail in St. Ann's Garrison. Explore exhibitions that include relics, works of art, and interactive displays, covering everything from the Amerindian era to the colonial period.

6. George Washington House: Visit George Washington House to immerse yourself in history. The first American president once stayed here when traveling to Barbados. This exquisitely preserved 18th-century home sheds light on Washington's existence and his relationship with Barbados. Learn more about the island's impact on young Washington by taking a guided tour.

7. Kensington Oval: One of the most prominent cricket fields in the Caribbean, Kensington Oval is a must-visit for cricket aficionados. This historic location has a long history of hosting international cricket games. Learn about the sport's importance in Barbados and the surrounding area by taking a tour.

8. Pebbles Beach: Located not far from Bridgetown, Pebbles Beach provides a peaceful respite from the bustle of the metropolis. The tranquil waves of this lovely beach are ideal for swimming and tanning. Coconut trees flank the beach, and beachside eateries provide delectable regional food and energizing beverages.

These are just a handful of Bridgetown, Barbados's major attractions. Whatever your interests (history, culture, outdoor recreation, or just relaxing on the beach), Bridgetown has plenty to offer.

Shopping and Dining in Bridgetown

Barbados's capital, Bridgetown, has a thriving and varied eating and retail scene. Here is a sample of the shopping and eating experiences you may have in Bridgetown, which range from crowded markets to elegant shops and from regional Bajan specialties to worldwide cuisine:

Shopping:

1. Broad Street: Broad Street is lined with a variety of shops, boutiques, and duty-free shops and serves as the city's primary shopping area. International fashion labels, jewelry, upscale products, and mementos are all available here. It's a fantastic location to shop for clothes, accessories, and one-of-a-kind presents.

2. Cheapside Market: At Cheapside Market, you may fully experience local culture. A vast variety of fresh vegetables, spices, regional crafts, and souvenirs are available at this bustling market. It's a wonderful location to enjoy the genuine tastes and hues of Barbados. taste tropical fruits, taste local foods, and peruse the market booths for one-of-a-kind handcrafted goods.

3. Pelican Craft Centre: This outlying Bridgetown attraction is a must-see for anybody who likes arts and crafts. This complex features traditional pottery, woodwork, jewelry, paintings, and other goods made by local artists. It's a fantastic location to find one-of-a-kind and genuine Barbadian souvenirs.

4. Limegrove Lifestyle Centre: In the adjacent village of Holetown, visit Limegrove Lifestyle Centre for a more affluent shopping experience. A variety of high-end apparel labels, fine jewelry, boutique shops, and art galleries are available at this opulent shopping destination. It's a terrific location for some shopping therapy and a variety of culinary experiences.

Dining:

1. Bajan Cuisines: Bridgetown is home to several restaurants serving delectable Bajan food, making it a gourmet haven. Don't pass up the opportunity to sample regional delicacies like flying fish, cou-cou (a dish made with cornmeal and okra), macaroni pie, pepperpot, and filling seafood meals. To experience

Barbados' genuine tastes, visit neighborhood restaurants and food stands.

2. Waterfront Restaurants: There are several eateries with stunning views and tasty seafood along the Careenage waterfront. Take in grilled fish, shrimp, lobster, and other Caribbean-inspired treats while dining with a view of the river. Numerous waterfront eateries also provide vibrant atmospheres and live music.

3. International Cuisine: Bridgetown's rich food scene offers something for every palate. Restaurants featuring foreign cuisine, including Italian, Indian, Chinese, Japanese, Mexican, and more, are readily available. There are many possibilities to sate your appetites, whether you're in the urge for pizza, sushi, curry, or tacos.

4. Rum Shops: Barbados is known for its rum, thus visiting a nearby rum store is in and of itself a cultural experience. These relaxed, neighborhood bars provide a laid-back setting where you can unwind while sipping on a range of rum-based drinks and mingling with locals. It's a fantastic chance to see Barbadian culture and partake of the local booze.

Bridgetown has something to please every pallet, whether you're seeking regional specialties, upmarket dining opportunities, or a taste of foreign food. The city provides a fascinating combination of eating and shopping experiences that will leave you yearning for more of Barbados' thriving culinary scene, from strolling through crowded markets to dining at seaside restaurants.

Nightlife Bridgetown

Barbados's main city, Bridgetown, comes to life at night with a thriving and energetic nightlife scene. Here are some highlights of Bridgetown's nightlife, which range from vibrant pubs and clubs to cultural events and live music:

1. St. Lawrence Gap: St. Lawrence Gap is a well-known nightlife destination around

Bridgetown. Numerous different pubs, nightclubs, and eateries line this busy boulevard. You may go between venues while taking in live performances, DJ sets, and soca, reggae, and calypso music sounds.

2. Harbour Lights: A famous outdoor nightclub that provides a distinctive party atmosphere, Harbour Lights is located on the seaside. It's a well-liked destination for both residents and tourists since it offers themed evenings, live entertainment, and a dance floor outside beneath the stars. Dance the night away while taking in the colorful ambiance and tropical beverages.

3. Oistins Fish Fry: The Oistins Fish Fry is a bustling street celebration that takes place every Friday night and features food, music, and dancing. A short distance from Bridgetown, Oistins is renowned for its flavorful environment and delicious fish. Enjoy mouthwatering fish and other Bajan dishes cooked to perfection, great music, and energizing street dancing.

4. Live Music and Entertainment: Bridgetown has several locations where you can take live music performances. At pubs, clubs, and cultural places, you may hear a variety of musical genres being performed, from reggae and soca to jazz and calypso. For experiences with live music, consider locations like The Waterfront Café, Blakey's on the Boardwalk, and Bert's Bar.

5. Mount Gay Rum Distillery Tour: If you like rum, you may want to go on a tour of the Mount Gay Rum Distillery. This historic distillery provides guided tours where visitors may discover the history of rum manufacturing in Barbados and sip on some of their well-known libations. It's a terrific way to start the evening before continuing your nighttime explorations.

6. Cultural Shows & Dinner Theaters: Enjoy dinner theater performances that include entertainment and a taste of Bajan food to learn more about the rich culture of Barbados. Enjoy tasty regional cuisine while watching performances of traditional music, dance, and theater. These programs provide a unique approach to experiencing Barbadian culture and entertainment.

7. Casinos: Bridgetown offers a few casinos where you may spend an evening of gaming and amusement if you want to try your luck. Try your luck at the slot machines or test your abilities at table games like poker, blackjack, and roulette. Additionally, some casinos organize unique events and live entertainment.

If you're searching for exciting clubs, live music, cultural activities, or just a laid-back evening at a seaside bar, Bridgetown's nightlife has something for everyone. You may discover a range of entertainment alternatives to suit your interests and make your evenings in Barbados unforgettable thanks to the city's thriving nightlife culture.

IV. DISCOVERING BARBADOS BEACHES

Barbados is well known for its breathtaking beaches, which have immaculate white sands, blue seas, and a variety of coastline vistas to discover. Here is a list of some of Barbados's top beaches, no matter whether you're looking for leisure, exciting water activities, or beautiful scenery:

Top Beaches in Barbados

Barbados is well known for its stunning beaches, each of which has its charm and attractions. The following list includes some of Barbados' top beaches that are worth visiting:

1. Crane Beach: Crane Beach, on the southeast coast, is often cited as one of the world's most magnificent beaches. It has imposing cliffs, a vivid blue ocean, and gentle pink dunes. The beach is a great place for picnics, sunning, and taking in the breathtaking view.

2. Miami Beach (Enterprise Beach): This popular destination is located on the southern coast close to Oistins. It has tranquil, clean seas, smooth beaches, and mild waves. With lifeguards on duty and amenities accessible, the beach is ideal for swimming and is family-friendly.

3. Bathsheba Beach: Bathsheba Beach, on the untamed east coast, is renowned for its impressive rock formations and strong Atlantic surf. With its difficult breakers and waves, it's a well-liked location for surfers. Visitors may savor the scenic surroundings, discover tidal pools, and take in exceptional natural beauty.

4. Carlisle Bay: Carlisle Bay, located on the southwest coast, is a gorgeous length of coastline that provides a mix of clean sandy beaches and fantastic snorkeling options.

Numerous shipwrecks in the area have created an underwater paradise for divers and snorkelers.

5. Bottom Bay: Secluded and scenic, with towering cliffs, fine sand, and crystal-clear seas, Bottom Bay is located on the southeast coast. It provides a serene environment ideal for unwinding and taking in Barbados' stunning scenery.

6. Mullins Beach: Mullins Beach, which lies on the west coast, is a busy and well-liked beach location. It provides an expansive stretch of golden sand, serene seas, and a lively environment. Visitors may partake in various water sports, dine on the beach, or just laze about.

7. Paynes Bay: A stunning beach famed for its pure seas and fine white sand, Paynes Bay is located on the west coast. It's a fantastic location for snorkeling, swimming, and sea turtle watching. Additionally, seaside eating and water sports are available to visitors.

8. Accra Beach: Rockley Beach, commonly known as Accra Beach, is a bustling and well-liked beach that is situated on the south coast. It has a broad sandy beach, calm waves, and some facilities including bars, restaurants, and places to rent beach chairs.

These are only a handful of Barbados' top beaches, each of which has its distinctive qualities and attractions. Barbados offers a beach for any desire, whether you're looking for leisure, water activities, or natural beauty. This will ensure that your tropical vacation is memorable.

Water Activities and Sports

Barbados is a haven for lovers of water sports and water-related activities because of its mild temperature and emerald seas. The best water sports and activities in Barbados range from exhilarating excursions to relaxing pleasures.

1. Snorkeling and Scuba Diving: Take a snorkeling or scuba diving excursion to discover Barbados' colorful underwater environment. The island is home to several shipwrecks, coral reefs, and other aquatic life. Carlisle Bay, Folkestone Marine Park, and the SS Stavronikita wreck are three well-liked diving locations. For all levels of expertise, there are diving and snorkeling trips available.

2. Jet Skiing: Take a jet ski ride and feel the rush of skimming through the waves. There are several locations in Barbados where you can hire jet skis and have thrilling coast rides. Feel the thrill of excitement as you travel through the beautiful seas while riding alone or with a guide.

3. Surfing: With waves that draw surfers from all over the globe, Barbados is a well-known surfing destination. For skilled surfers, the east shore of the island, notably Soup Bowl near Bathsheba, delivers reliable and strong waves. There are surf schools that provide instruction and equipment rentals for beginners.

4. Stand-up Paddleboarding (SUP): Stand-up Paddleboarding (SUP) is a great way to explore Barbados' tranquil seas. SUP is a well-liked and soothing sport that lets you float around the beach, take in the marine life, and take in the stunning scenery. Numerous beaches and water sports facilities offer SUP rentals and guided trips.

5. Sailing and Catamaran Cruises: Take a sailing excursion or go on a catamaran trip to see Barbados' beauty from the ocean. Take a leisurely trip around the coast, go snorkeling in remote coves, and relax on the deck. Additionally, some cruises include food, beverages, and entertainment on board.

6. Fishing: Anglers will find Barbados to be a paradise. To increase your chances of catching marlin, sailfish, tuna, and other game fish, go fishing on a charter. You may schedule deep-sea fishing outings as half-day or full-day excursions with professional guides at your side.

7. Kayaking and Paddleboarding: Kayak or paddleboard your way around Barbados' coastline at your speed. A coastal experience may be had by renting a kayak or paddleboard and exploring quiet beaches, mangroves, and secret coves. For anyone interested in learning more about the island's marine ecosystems, guided trips are also offered.

8. Kiteboarding and Windsurfing: Barbados is a great location for kiteboarding and windsurfing due to its consistent trade winds and ideal conditions. If you want to surf the waves with your kite or sail, go to Silver Rock Beach or Long Beach.

These are just a handful of the many water sports and activities Barbados offers. The island provides a variety of possibilities to satisfy the needs of any water enthusiast, whether they are looking for excitement, leisure, or a chance to explore the underwater world.

Beach Safety Tips

It's crucial to put safety first while visiting Barbados' stunning beaches to guarantee a pleasant and incident-free trip. Following are some recommendations for beach safety:

1. Swim at Beaches With Lifeguards On Duty: Whenever feasible, go swimming at beaches with lifeguards on duty. They are skilled in spotting possible dangers and offering quick support in an emergency.

2. Be Aware of Water Conditions: Keep an eye out for things like rip currents, strong currents, and choppy waves. Pay attention to warning flags and signage, and stay out of the water in certain places. Ask a lifeguard for guidance if you're unsure.

3. Swim with Caution: Before you go in the water, evaluate your swimming prowess, and never swim by yourself. Swim in authorized locations and stay close to the shoreline. Watch out for abrupt drops off and uneven seabeds.

4. Stay Hydrated: Due to Barbados' tropical environment, which may be hot and muggy, it's crucial to drink enough water. Avoid dehydration by drinking plenty of water, particularly if you're exercising or spending a lot of time in the sun.

5. Protect Your Skin: To shield your skin from the sun's damaging rays, use sunscreen with a high SPF (sun protection factor). Regularly reapply sunscreen, particularly after swimming or perspiring. To protect oneself from the sun, put on caps, clothes, and sunglasses.

6. Respect Marine Life: When snorkeling or swimming, show consideration for marine life by not harming or upsetting corals, fish, or other aquatic organisms. Avoid feeding or chasing them and instead admire them from a distance.

7. Respect Your Limits: Take part in water sports and activities that are appropriate for your skill level and physical capabilities. To protect your safety while starting a new hobby, enroll in courses or consult with experts.

8. Keep an Eye on Kids: If you're taking kids to the beach, keep a tight eye on them at all times. When swimming, keep kids within reach at all times, and life jackets or flotation devices may contribute to their security.

9. Pay Attention to Weather Changes: Pay attention to the weather and the forecast. When there are thunderstorms or other bad weather conditions, seek cover and stay out of the water.

10. Follow Beach Rules and Regulations: Respect any posted laws and limitations at the beach, such as warnings against diving, restrictions on the speed of boats, and bans on fires and alcohol consumption. These guidelines are in place to protect you and the beach's natural ecosystem.

By putting your safety and the safety of those around you first, you can take advantage of your time in Barbados, soak up the sun, and have a wonderful beach experience.

V. EXPLORING THE NATURAL BEAUTY OF BARBADOS

Barbados is renowned for its unique natural beauty in addition to its beautiful beaches. There are many possibilities to immerse yourself in the island's natural beauties, from lush tropical gardens to spectacular caverns and tranquil nature reserves. Here are some methods to discover Barbados' stunning natural surroundings:

National Parks and Reserves

Despite being a tiny island, Barbados has several national parks and reserves that highlight the country's unique ecosystems and natural beauty. These protected areas provide possibilities for hiking, animal viewing, and taking in the quiet of the outdoors. Here are some noteworthy Barbados parks and reserves:

1. Graeme Hall Nature Sanctuary: Graeme Hall Nature Sanctuary is a privately-owned reserve devoted to the protection of wetland ecosystems, and it is situated on the south coast of Barbados. Many different bird species, such as herons, egrets, and migratory birds, call it home. Visitors may stroll along the boardwalk pathways, discover the value of wetland ecosystems, and take in the area's abundant wildlife.

2. Andromeda Botanic Gardens: This tranquil and beautiful botanical park is located on the eastern shore of the island. There is a variety of tropical flora there, including uncommon and unusual species. Wanderers may enjoy the tranquil atmosphere while taking in the vibrant blossoms and verdant landscapes. Additionally, the gardens provide breathtaking views of the Atlantic Ocean.

3. Welchman Hall Gully: Welchman Hall Gully, a natural marvel with a deep tropical ravine, is situated in the center of Barbados. The gully is home to a variety of animals, including green monkeys, as well as rich foliage, tall trees, and other species. Visitors may stroll along the gully's twisting pathways, viewing native species and taking in the peace of this unique habitat.

4. Animal Flower Cave: A sea cave at the island's northernmost point, Animal Flower Cave is renowned for its unspoiled beauty and breathtaking coastline vistas. The cave has chambers with crystal-clear pools of water and unusual rock formations. Visitors may take a guided tour, discover the geology of the cave, and, depending on the weather, swim in the pools.

5. Chancery Lane Wetland Reserve: This protected area on the south coast is home to several bird species and other animals. The reserve's mangroves, ponds, and freshwater marshes serve as an essential environment for wildlife. Species including herons, kingfishers, and sandpipers may be seen by birdwatchers.

6. Farley Hill National Park: This park, which is located in the parish of St. Peter, is home to a historic plantation mansion and lovely gardens. The park has well-kept pathways that are perfect for strolls and picnics among the picturesque scenery. The lofty position of the park offers sweeping views of the countryside and the shore.

The island's natural treasures, the island's ecosystems, and tranquil moments in nature may all be enjoyed by visitors to Barbados' national parks and reserves. These protected places provide a view into the varied and distinctive natural heritage of Barbados, whether it is via botanical garden exploration, animal observation, or enjoying the peace of wetland environments.

Hiking and Nature Trails

Barbados is renowned for its beautiful beaches, but it also has wonderful hiking and nature paths that let tourists discover the island's varied landscapes and unspoiled beauty. There are alternatives to satisfy any hiker, whether they choose seaside hikes, woodland routes, or picturesque vistas. The following hiking and wildlife routes are well-known in Barbados:

1. Barbados National Trust Hikes: The Barbados National Trust arranges frequent treks that lead you into the island's natural treasures and off the beaten path. These escorted hikes cover a variety of landscapes, including historical buildings, luscious valleys, and coastal cliffs. The Moonlight Walk at Gun Hill Signal Station and the Welchman Hall Gully trek are two popular hikes.

2. East Coast Hiking Trail: This trail follows Barbados' wild and beautiful east coast and provides breathtaking vistas of the Atlantic Ocean. From St. John Parish Church, a route leads to Bathsheba via picturesque countryside and seaside communities. Along the trip, hikers may see impressive cliffs, hidden bays, and quaint fishing villages.

3. Welchman Hall Gully Hike: This tropical ravine in the island's center is home to a wide variety of plants and wildlife. The gully offers well-kept pathways that run through dense foliage for a natural experience. The tall trees, local vegetation, and green monkeys may all be seen by hikers as they take in the scenery.

4. Farley Hill National Park Trails: Located in St. Peter Parish, Farley Hill National Park has walking paths that meander through lovely gardens and wooded regions. The park's pathways provide an opportunity to explore the remnants of an old plantation home, see the well-kept lawns, and take in the tranquility of the surrounding landscape.

5. Scotland District Hiking Trails: The northeastern region of the island's Scotland District is renowned for its picturesque beauty and mountainous topography. Rolling hills, little towns, and scenic landscapes are all crossed by the hiking paths in this region. The paths provide expansive vistas of the shore and the chance to find off-the-beaten-path treasures.

6. Flower Forest Nature Trails: The Flower Forest, located in Barbados's center, is a well-kept nature walk that meanders through beautiful tropical foliage and gardens. Hikers may take pleasure in the tranquil atmosphere, adore the colorful blossoms, and savor the expansive views of the East Coast and the surrounding countryside.

Walks through the well-preserved tropical forest are available at the Barbados Wildlife Reserve, which lies on the island's northwest coast. While strolling along the authorized routes within the reserve, visitors may see local wildlife such as green monkeys, tortoises, and colorful birds.

It's important to pack the right gear, sun protection, enough water, and a map or guidebook before starting any trip. It's also a good idea to let someone know your intentions and trek throughout the day. Barbados offers fantastic opportunities for hikers to interact with nature and uncover the island's hidden jewels thanks to its diverse paths and breathtaking landscape.

Wildlife and Marine Life

Barbados is recognized for its abundant biodiversity and marine life in addition to its stunning beaches and lively culture. On land and in the nearby seas, the island provides a wide variety of possibilities to see intriguing animals. Here is a list of the types of animals and aquatic life you may see in Barbados:

Land Wildlife:
1. Green Monkeys: Barbados is well-known for its green monkey population. These amusing and inquisitive monkeys are spread over the island, including gullies and natural preserves. As you explore the beautiful surroundings of Barbados, keep an eye out for them.

2. Birds: With over 200 kinds of birds living on or visiting the island, Barbados is a sanctuary for birdwatchers. Bird aficionados will find much to see and appreciate, from vibrant tropical birds like the Barbados Bullfinch and Red-legged Thrush to migratory species like the Snowy Egret and American Kestrel.

3. Sea Turtles: Several species of sea turtles, including the severely endangered Leatherback turtle and the endangered Hawksbill turtle, make Barbados home. These magnificent animals may be nesting or hatching on the island's beaches, particularly along the east coast. Visitors may see and take part in turtle conservation efforts via certain planned excursions and conservation programs.

Marine Species:
1. Coral Reefs: The huge coral reefs that encircle Barbados are home to a diverse range of marine species. You may witness vibrant coral formations, tropical fish, and other reef inhabitants like sea fans, sponges, and crabs while snorkeling or scuba diving in these clear waters.

2. Tropical Fish: The colorful tropical fish that abound in Barbados' seas make snorkeling and diving excursions there really unforgettable. Watch out for animals that bring colorful splashes to the underwater environment, such as butterflyfish, angelfish, parrotfish, and sergeant majors.

3. Sea Turtles: In addition to coming ashore to lay their eggs, sea turtles may also be seen when diving or snorkeling. Sea turtles live in Barbados' warm seas as well as those who come to visit. Swim next to these kinds of animals and see their exquisite movements in their natural environment.

4. Marine Mammals: Although fewer frequent visitors, marine mammals do sometimes stop by Barbados. Offshore, dolphins and whales have been seen, including the Spinner Dolphin, Bottlenose Dolphin, and Humpback Whale. You may see more of these amazing animals on boat trips designed exclusively for marine mammal observation.

5. Shipwrecks: Barbados is home to many ships that have been transformed into artificial reefs that serve as homes for marine life. These wrecks are home to a variety of fish species and other marine animals, which divers might meet while exploring these underwater locations.

Barbados provides a wide variety of animal and marine life interactions, whether you want to explore the island's woods and gullies on land or scuba dive in the surrounding seas. Future generations will be able to continue to appreciate Barbados' natural beauty and biodiversity as long as these natural assets are respected and preserved.

Botanical Gardens

Several magnificent botanical gardens can be found in Barbados, which highlight the island's vast plant variety and provide tourists with a calm retreat into nature. These gardens provide the opportunity to learn about the island's flora as well as a range of exotic and native plant species, lovely groomed landscapes, etc. Check out these well-known botanical gardens in Barbados:

1. Andromeda Botanic Gardens: This attraction is a must-see for plant aficionados and is situated at St. Joseph on the eastern coast of the island. This six-acre tropical paradise has a huge variety of plants from all over the globe. While strolling among the lush vegetation, colorful blossoms, and tranquil ponds, visitors may enjoy the routes' winding walkways. The grounds give breathtaking views of the shoreline and make a beautiful setting for a stroll.

2. Hunte's Gardens: A secret treasure developed by horticulturalist Anthony Hunte, Hunte's Gardens is tucked away in the hills of St. Joseph. This magical garden has a variety of tropical flora, enormous trees, and winding paths. Wandering around the shady corners and colorful flower beds, visitors may look for hidden sculptures and take in the tranquil atmosphere. For those who like the outdoors, Hunte's Gardens provides a unique and whimsical experience.

3. Flower Forest: The Flower Forest, a botanical area with a stunning display of tropical flowers and plants, is located in the island's center. The 53-acre garden has a varied assortment of palms, orchids, heliconias, and other vibrant blossoms. Explore the well-kept pathways that run through the woodland and provide sweeping views of the East Coast and the surroundings.

4. Welchman Hall Gully: Although Welchman Hall Gully is not precisely a botanical garden, it is a natural marvel that enables visitors to fully immerse themselves in a lush tropical setting. Numerous plant species, including ferns, palms, and tropical trees, may be found in this gully. Visitors may take in the towering foliage, take in the sounds of nature, and get a sight of green monkeys swinging through the trees while strolling along the shady trails.

These Barbados botanical gardens provide a lovely mix of untouched landscapes, horticultural know-how, and tranquil settings. These gardens provide a chance to admire the island's varied flora and immerse yourself in the alluring world of Barbadian botany, whether you are a plant expert, a nature lover, or just looking for a quiet getaway.

VI. HISTORICAL AND CULTURAL SITES

There are several historical and cultural landmarks in Barbados, an energetic island with a rich history and cultural legacy, which provide insights into the island's past and present. There are many locations to visit and learn about the interesting history and varied culture of Barbados, from colonial landmarks to museums and cultural institutions. These prominent historical and cultural locations may be found in Barbados:

Historical Plantations and Museums

There are several historical plantations and museums in Barbados that provide insight into the island's plantation period and its influence on its history and culture. These locations provide an opportunity to learn about Barbados's sugar business, plantation life, and influential individuals. The following historical plantations and museums may be found in Barbados:

1. St. Nicholas Abbey: Located in Barbados, St. Nicholas Abbey is a notable historical monument and one of the oldest plantation homes in the Caribbean. This Jacobean home in St. Peter Parish offers a glimpse into 17th-century plantation life. The beautifully-preserved home is open for visitors to tour, as well as the neighboring sugar cane fields and old furniture and antiquities. Visitors may taste and buy the plantation's rum, which it also makes.

2. Sunbury Plantation House: This is a beautifully restored plantation house that serves as a reminder of Barbados' colonial past. It is located in St. Philip Parish. The house, which dates back to the 17th century and is filled with antiques including furniture, china, and works of art, offers a glimpse into plantation life at the time. Well-kept gardens, a courtyard with a collection of carriages, and a restaurant serving regional food can be found on the grounds surrounding the building.

3. Morgan Lewis Windmill: As Barbados' last remaining sugar windmill, Morgan Lewis Windmill serves as a representation of the island's sugar trade. Visitors can see the equipment and procedures used to grind sugar cane at this historic site in St. Andrew Parish. Learn about the historical significance of sugar production in Barbados by ascending to the windmill's summit, where you'll also get sweeping views of the surrounding countryside.

4. The Barbados Museum and Historical Society: The Barbados Museum and Historical Society, located in a former British military prison in Bridgetown, offers a thorough overview of the island's history and culture. The museum displays a wide variety of artifacts, such as Amerindian artifacts, remnants from the colonial era, and works of local artists. It provides insight into several historical facets of Barbados, including the slave trade, the sugar industry, and the growth of the island's social and cultural fabric.

5. Arlington House Museum: This museum, which is situated in Speightstown, immerses visitors in Barbadian history. The museum, located in a restored 18th-century structure, offers interactive displays that highlight the island's history, from its Amerindian origins to the present. Discover the history of the sugar industry, look around the exhibits, and take in the expansive views of the city from the rooftop terrace.

6. Barbados Concorde Experience: Conveniently located close to Grantley Adams International Airport, the Barbados Concorde Experience offers a singular chance to learn about the Concorde, the sole supersonic passenger plane in existence. Step aboard the actual aircraft to experience the luxury and technology of this iconic plane, take in interactive exhibits that explore the history of the Concorde and its influence on travel, and more.

These historical plantations and museums in Barbados give visitors a look into the island's past, especially the time when sugar was produced and life was lived on plantations. They offer educational and immersive experiences, helping visitors to obtain a greater knowledge of Barbados' history, culture, and the legacy left by its plantation past.

UNESCO World Heritage Sites

Two UNESCO World Heritage Sites that highlight the cultural and historical importance of the island are something Barbados is proud of. These locations, which have been honored by UNESCO for their exceptional universal worth, are a must-see for anybody interested in learning about Barbados' history. Barbados has the following UNESCO World Heritage Sites:

1. Historic Bridgetown and its Garrison: This World Heritage Site includes Bridgetown's capital city and the surrounding Garrison neighborhood. Bridgetown is a thriving city with a lengthy history, and the buildings and other relics from that period have been kept effectively. During the colonial era, the fortified military structure known as the Garrison sector was essential to the island's security. They stand for the island's history of colonization, commerce, and armed conflict together. Visit the Parliament Buildings and St. Michael's Cathedral, stroll through Bridgetown's quaint streets, and learn about the island's history in the museums and historical sites that make up this UNESCO World Historical Site.

2. The Parliament Buildings of Barbados: The Parliament Buildings, which are situated in Bridgetown, is a crucial component of the UNESCO World Heritage Site known as Historic Bridgetown and its Garrison. These structures—the Parliament House and the Public Buildings—reflect Barbados' political past and democratic institutions. They are recognizable monuments. Government offices are located at the Public Buildings, while the island's legislature is housed in the Parliament House. Learn about the country's political history and see the stunning architecture.

These Barbados UNESCO World Heritage Sites provide a chance to learn about the island's history, discover its architectural gems, and comprehend its importance. These locations, which range from colonial structures to military strongholds, showcase the rich historical and cultural legacy of Barbados. Immerse yourself in the past, take a walk around the streets, and be grateful that these significant sites that have contributed to Barbados' character are being preserved.

Cultural and Art Festivals

Barbados is a thriving center of culture and art, and the island is well-known for its exciting celebrations of many creative mediums via festivals and other events. There are several festivals and cultural events held all year long that highlight the originality and ability of

Barbadian and foreign artists in everything from music and dance to visual arts and literature. Here are a few of Barbados' most famous artistic and cultural events:

1. Barbados Jazz Festival: The Barbados Jazz Festival, which takes place in January, is eagerly anticipated by jazz fans. The festival hosts a series of concerts and performances including both national and international jazz performers at several locations across the island. Enjoy jazz's silky melodies, heartfelt songs, and contagious rhythms in a tropical environment.

2. Crop Over Festival: The Crop Over Festival, one of Barbados' most well-known cultural occasions, is a lively celebration that concludes the sugar cane harvesting season. From June through August, a variety of events are held during this six-week festival, including vibrant parades, exciting calypso, and soca music contests, displays of costume creation, and delectable Bajan food. The Grand Kadooment Day, a stunning street parade when revelers dress in extravagant costumes and dance to throbbing beats, serves as the festival's grand finale.

3. Holetown Festival: To honor the 1627 arrival of the first English settlers in Barbados, the Holetown Festival is a yearly celebration celebrated in February. This week-long festival is held in the historic neighborhood of Holetown and includes some artistic and cultural activities, such as live music concerts, artisan fairs, street fairs, historical reenactments, and delectable cuisine. During this vibrant festival, you may learn about Barbados' rich legacy and sense of community.

4. Barbados Visual Arts Festival: The Barbados Visual Arts Festival, which takes place in November and involves exhibits, workshops, art lectures, and interactive art experiences, is devoted to exhibiting the visual arts sector in Barbados. It offers a venue for regional and international artists to showcase their creations and interact with the audience. The festival presents a wide variety of creative expressions, from painting and sculpture to photography and mixed media.

5. NIFCA (National Independence Festival of Creative Arts): NIFCA is an annual festival that highlights the creativity of Barbadians in a variety of creative mediums, including music, dance, theater, literary arts, visual arts, and craft. The festival, which runs from September through November, uses performances, exhibits, and contests to highlight the skills of both up-and-coming and seasoned artists. It gives artists a stage on which to share their creative concepts and enhance Barbados' cultural environment.

These cultural and artistic events in Barbados give chances to interact with a variety of artistic mediums and cultural expressions as well as a window into the island's thriving creative landscape. These festivals provide remarkable experiences that honor the creative prowess and cultural legacy of the island, whether you are a fan of music, an art aficionado, or just want to immerse yourself in Barbados' vibrant atmosphere.

Local Cuisine and Culinary Experiences

Barbados is a paradise because of its mouthwatering regional food as well as its stunning beaches and lively culture. Barbadian cuisine is a reflection of the island's varied background and is influenced by tastes from Africa, Britain, India, and the Creole region. Barbados provides a variety of culinary experiences that are guaranteed to delight your taste buds, from delectable seafood meals to substantial stews and savory street cuisine. The following are some highlights of Barbados' regional cuisine and culinary experiences:

1. Flying Fish and Cou Cou: A must-try culinary experience is flying fish and cou cou, which is regarded as the national dish of Barbados. A common way to serve flying fish, a mainstay of Barbadian cuisine, is to pan-fry it after mildly seasoning it. The cou cou, a delicacy made of cornmeal and okra, is eaten with fish. This mouthwatering combo highlights the island's appreciation of local foods and fresh fish.

2. Macaroni Pie: A cheesy baked pasta dish that is a popular comfort food in Barbados, macaroni pie is often served as a side dish with meals. This creamy and delicious treat is popular among both residents and tourists. It is made with macaroni, cheese, eggs, and other spices.

3. Pudding and Souse: In Barbados, pudding and souse is a customary Saturday supper meal. In contrast to souse, which consists of pickled meats like pork or other meats, pudding is a spicy black pudding produced from pig's blood and numerous spices. A lovely blend of acidic and savory sensations is produced by this distinctive flavor combination.

4. Bajan Pepper Sauce: Trying the renowned Bajan pepper sauce is a must-do when visiting Barbados. This spicy sauce is tasty and made with Scotch bonnet peppers, mustard, vinegar, and spices. It is a common spice that gives many Barbadian foods a fiery bite, and you can find it on tables all across the island.

5. Fish Fry at Oistins: On Barbados' south coast, Oistins Fish Fry offers a colorful dining experience. Locals and guests come together for an evening of great music, dancing, and delicious seafood at this exciting Friday night event. Enjoy great seafood alternatives including grilled fish, lobster, shrimp, and other seafood in a buzzy setting with dynamic entertainment.

6. Rum Tastings and Distillery Tours: Barbados is well-known for its rum, and a trip to the island isn't complete without trying some of the best brands. Visit a rum distillery, such as Mount Gay or St. Nicholas Abbey, for a tour to understand how rum is made and to sample a variety of aged rums. Learn more about the distinctive character of Barbados' diverse tastes.

7. Street Food Delights: Discover Barbados' thriving street food scene, where you may sample a variety of regional specialties. Try traditional dishes like fish cakes, cutters (fish or pork-stuffed sandwiches), rotis (flatbreads with an Indian flair filled with curried meats or vegetables), and conkies (sweet desserts made of cornmeal and coconut wrapped in banana leaves). These delicious street foods are ideal for a fast snack and provide a sample of Barbados' diverse culinary offerings.

Barbados provides a culinary experience that will tickle your taste buds and leave you wanting more, whether you enjoy indulging in seafood delicacies, savoring traditional Bajan meals, or discovering the island's street food culture. Barbados is a genuine food lover's paradise, so embrace the tastes, immerse yourself in the regional cuisine, and relish the mouthwatering gastronomic experiences.

VII. SPORTS AND RECREATION

Barbados is a great location for outdoor enthusiasts and sports fans since it provides a broad variety of sports and leisure activities. There are several choices to keep guests engaged and active, including both water sports and land-based pursuits. You may enjoy the following sports and leisure pursuits in Barbados:

Diving and Water Sports

Divers and fans of water sports will both find paradise in Barbados. The island provides an exceptional experience for those wishing to explore the underwater world and enjoy exhilarating aquatic adventures thanks to its pristine seas, colorful marine life, and a selection of water sports. Here are some of Barbados' most well-liked water sports and diving opportunities:

1. Snorkeling: Snorkeling is a great opportunity to explore the vibrant coral reefs and take in the variety of marine life that resides in the seas around Barbados. The reefs off the west and south coastlines, Carlisle Bay, and Folkestone Marine Park are a few of the greatest places to go snorkeling. To explore Barbados' underwater splendor, you may rent snorkeling equipment or sign up for a guided snorkeling excursion.

2. Scuba Diving: Barbados is known for its top-notch scuba diving locations. There are dive facilities and operators that provide a variety of diving experiences, whether you are an experienced diver or a novice trying to become certified. Visit vivid coral reefs, interesting shipwrecks, and marine life including turtles, rays, and tropical fish. Carlisle Bay Marine Park,

SS Stavronikita, and the Pamir are a few well-liked diving locations.

3. Jet Skiing: Experience the rush of speeding across Barbados' crystal-clear waters on a jet ski. By renting a jet ski, you may freely cruise the shoreline, negotiate waves, and go on thrilling waterborne adventures. Jet ski rentals and escorted trips are provided by several rental companies, guaranteeing a fun and safe experience.

4. Windsurfing and Kitesurfing: Barbados is a great location for windsurfing and kitesurfing due to its constant trade winds. Go to Silver Rock Beach on the south coast, which is renowned for its consistent winds and ideal weather. You may take lessons, rent gear, and feel the rush of gliding through the waves whether you're a novice or an expert rider.

5. Stand-Up Paddleboarding (SUP): This enjoyable water sport has gained popularity all over the globe, and Barbados is the ideal location to try it out. Engage your core muscles and take in the tranquility of the ocean as you glide past quiet bays, discover secret coves, and take in a unique viewpoint of the coastline.

6. Deep-Sea Fishing: In the abounding seas around Barbados, anglers may board deep-sea fishing cruises and try their luck. Go out to sea with knowledgeable instructors who will show you the best fishing locations. While taking in the stunning ocean views, catch marlin, tuna, wahoo, and other game species.

7. Catamaran Cruises: Take a catamaran tour to see Barbados' stunning coastline. Enjoy the amazing views of the island from the ocean as you unwind on the balcony and soak up the sun. The best approach to combine water sports with relaxation is to take a catamaran cruise, which often offers snorkeling chances, onboard entertainment, and delectable meals.

Barbados provides a wide range of water sports and diving activities to suit all interests and ability levels, whether you're looking for undersea exploration, high-speed water adventures, or a relaxing cruise along the coast. The island guarantees water aficionados a wonderful experience with its warm seas, rich marine life, and qualified staff.

Golfing in Barbados

Barbados is a golfer's dream with top-notch golf courses situated among breathtaking tropical scenery. Barbados has several championship golf courses that can accommodate players of all skill levels, whether you're an experienced player or a novice wishing to enjoy a leisurely game. An overview of golf in Barbados is provided below:

1. Sandy Lane Golf Club: The Sandy Lane Golf Club is renowned for its grandeur and elegance and is situated on Barbados's prominent west coast. The Old Nine, The Country Club, and The Green Monkey are three of the club's difficult courses. These golf courses, which were created by well-known designers like Tom Fazio and Robert Trent Jones Jr., include breathtaking vistas, lush fairways, and spotless greens. The Sandy Lane Golf Club welcomes golf aficionados from all over the globe and has played home to important competitions.

2. Apes Hill Club: The Apes Hill Club, a magnificent golf course with sweeping views of Barbados' stunning landscape and shoreline, is tucked away in the island's hills. The course's stunning greens, natural gullies, and dramatic elevation changes were all part of Chris Cole's design. The superb golfing experience offered by Apes Hill Club is enhanced by opulent facilities and friendly Bajan friendliness.

3. Royal Westmoreland Golf Club: Located on the west coast of Barbados, the 18-hole championship course at the Royal Westmoreland Golf Club was created by famous golf architect Robert Trent Jones Jr. The course's lush fairways, tough bunkers, and breathtaking vistas of the Caribbean Sea are all part of its exquisite landscaping. Royal Westmoreland provides a top-notch golfing experience with its first-rate amenities and a magnificent clubhouse.

4. Barbados Golf Club: Situated in the south of the island, this public course is open to players of all skill levels. The course was created by Ron Kirby and has broad fairways, strategically positioned bunkers, and wavy greens. Both residents and tourists choose the Barbados Golf Club because of its laid-back and welcoming attitude.

5. Rockley Golf Course: The nine-hole, par-35 Rockley Golf Course is located on Barbados' south coast and offers players a pleasant and difficult experience. The course provides a tranquil atmosphere as it is surrounded by lush flora and tropical flowers. A driving range, putting green, and a clubhouse with a pro shop and restaurant are additional amenities at Rockley Golf Course.

6. Other Courses: In addition to the courses listed above, Barbados is home to several renowned golf courses, including the Barbados Royal Golf Club, which has breathtaking ocean vistas, and the difficult and picturesque Almond Beach Resort Golf Course.

When playing golf in Barbados, you can mix your passion for the game with the stunning scenery and friendly locals. Whether you want a well-known championship course or a more relaxed one, Barbados provides a wide variety of golfing experiences. Pack your clubs, take in the wind from the Caribbean, and tee off in paradise.

Cricket and Other Sports

Cricket is the national sport of Barbados and has a unique position in Barbadian culture. The island has a long history of cricket and has produced numerous players of international renown. Cricket matches are not merely athletic competitions; they are also community-building social activities. The Kensington Oval in Bridgetown, which has played home to many international games and is regarded as one of the best cricket grounds in the Caribbean, is the most recognizable cricket venue in Barbados.

In addition to cricket, Barbados provides a variety of other sports and leisure pursuits for residents and guests to take part in. Here are a few of Barbados' preferred sports:

1. Football (soccer): Football is a popular sport in Barbados and is highly watched there. There are several professional and amateur leagues, clubs, and tournaments on the island, which are all governed by the Barbados Football Association.

2. Netball: In Barbados, ladies enjoy playing the team sport of netball. For players of all ages and ability levels, the Barbados Netball Association hosts leagues and tournaments.

3. Basketball: Basketball has become more well-liked in Barbados, where more players and teams are taking part in leagues and competitions there. On the island, basketball is governed by the Barbados Amateur Basketball Association.

4. Tennis: Barbados has a vibrant tennis scene, and the island is home to both public and private tennis courts. Tennis courts are often offered to visitors at resorts and hotels. Tennis programs and tournaments are promoted and planned by the Barbados Tennis Association for players of all ages.

5. Horse Racing: In Barbados, horse racing is a well-liked activity, and the Garrison Savannah racetrack in Bridgetown serves as the primary location for competitions. The famous Sandy Lane Gold Cup is only one of the events that the Barbados Turf Club sponsors throughout the year.

6. Surfing: The east coast of Barbados is recognized for having great surfing conditions. A well-known surf location in Bathsheba called The Soup Bowl draws surfers from all over the globe. In Barbados' warm seas, surfers may catch the waves and experience the rush of the sport.

7. Road Cycling and Running: The beautiful roads and comfortable weather on Barbados are attracting a rising number of road cyclists and runners. Both athletes and spectators are drawn to events like the Run Barbados Marathon Weekend and different cycling competitions.

These are only a few examples of the sports and leisure pursuits accessible in Barbados. Beyond this, the island offers chances for swimming, cricket, track and field, sailing, and other activities. Barbados has a thriving sports culture that appeals to a variety of interests and passions, whether you're an athlete or a spectator.

Wellness and Spa Retreats

Visitors wishing to rest and care for their well-being will find a variety of health and spa resorts in Barbados to be reviving and pleasant. The island is the perfect place to engage in spa services, yoga courses, meditation sessions, and other wellness pursuits thanks to its serene surroundings, stunning beaches, and opulent lodgings. Here are a few of Barbados' health and spa getaway options:

1. Luxury Resorts and Hotels: Barbados is home to several opulent resorts and hotels, many of which include first-rate wellness centers and spas that provide a broad variety of treatments and services. The pampering options available to visitors range from holistic treatments to revitalizing massages, all of which are intended to promote relaxation and well-being. Sandy Lane, The Crane Resort, and Cobblers Cove are a few well-known Barbados resorts.

2. Boutique Wellness Retreats: Several boutique wellness retreats in Barbados provide a more individualized and private experience. These retreats often include customized programs including holistic therapies, yoga, meditation, wellness courses, and nutritious food. They are created to encourage equilibrium, awareness, and general well-being. There are retreats available all year long at locations like Yellow Bird Yoga, Santosha Yoga Camp, and Zen Sanctuary.

3. Beachfront Yoga and Meditation: Barbados' gorgeous beaches and peaceful environment provide it the ideal location for beachside yoga and meditation sessions. Yoga and meditation sessions are often provided on the sand by hotels and independent teachers, enabling students to commune with nature, unwind, and enhance their general well-being.

4. Wellness Retreats and Workshops: Barbados conducts several wellness retreats, seminars, and workshops all year long. For the benefit of attendees, these events often bring together professionals in disciplines like yoga, nutrition, fitness, and mindfulness. It's a chance to discover new techniques, acquire insightful knowledge, and interact with others who share your goals for well-being.

5. Spa and Wellness Packages: A lot of Barbados' spas and wellness facilities provide packages that bring together various treatments and services for a comprehensive and opulent experience. Visitors may customize their spa packages to meet their requirements and tastes, choosing from massages and facials to body cleanses and detox treatments.

6. Natural Healing Therapies: Barbados is renowned for its abundant natural resources, and several resorts and health retreats make use of the medicinal properties of the island. Visitors may benefit from natural therapeutic modalities that are strongly ingrained in the island's culture, from blending traditional techniques like aromatherapy and herbal cures into treatments to using local plant elements in cosmetic products.

7. Fitness and Outdoor Activities: Barbados provides a variety of outdoor activities and fitness opportunities to improve general well-being in addition to spa services and relaxation. Visitors may partake in physical activities that refresh both the body and the mind, such as beachside exercises, nature treks, swimming, and water sports.

Barbados offers a range of alternatives to suit your requirements, whether you're searching for a tranquil retreat to rest in or want to start a wellness journey. The island's health and spa services, which range from opulent resorts to private retreats, guarantee a restorative experience that will leave you feeling renewed, balanced, and rejuvenated.

VIII. ISLAND EXCURSIONS

Barbados provides a wide range of intriguing island excursions for travelers to discover and enjoy, with its varied landscapes and rich cultural history. There is something for everyone, whether your interests are in historical landmarks, natural marvels, or a thriving local culture. Here are a few well-liked island outings in Barbados:

1. Island Tours: A fantastic approach to learning about Barbados' top attractions is to take an island tour. These excursions often include historical sites like Bridgetown's Garrison, Bathsheba on the east coast, Harrison's Cave, and picturesque coastal regions including the craggy Atlantic coast and breathtaking west coast beaches. Insights about the island's history, culture, and natural beauty are offered by knowledgeable guides.

2. Wildlife and Nature Reserves: The island of Barbados is home to several reserves for wildlife and an environment where you may see unusual plants and animals. Visit locations like the Barbados Wildlife Reserve to witness species like green monkeys in their natural environment. Another must-see is Hunte's Gardens, which has beautifully groomed gardens and a huge assortment of tropical plants and flowers.

3. Historical Plantations: Barbados is home to some historic plantations that provide a window into the colonial history of the island. For instance, St. Nicholas Abbey is a 17th-century plantation mansion that has been exquisitely kept. Visitors may take a tour of the home, meander around the grounds, and discover the island's past involvement in the sugar business. The Sunbury Plantation House and the Morgan

Lewis Windmill are two further noteworthy plantations worth seeing.

4. Rum Distillery Tours: Barbados is known for its rum, therefore rum lovers must pay a visit to one of the island's rum distilleries. Visit the Mount Gay Rum Distillery, which has been creating rum since 1703, to learn about the production process and taste some of the best spirits the island has to offer. Tours and tastings are also available at St. Nicholas Abbey and the Foursquare Rum Distillery.

5. Oistins Fish Fry: Every Friday night, the renowned Oistins Fish Fry brings the fishing town of Oistins to life. Come enjoy an evening of mouth watering fresh seafood, live music, dancing, and a vibrant environment with the residents and guests alike. It's a wonderful opportunity to experience Bajan's friendliness and the local culture.

6. Underground Adventures: Visit sites like Harrison's Cave to learn more about Barbados' underground environment. Experience the breathtaking limestone structures, waterfalls, and pools of the cave on a guided tram trip. On the island's northernmost point, the Animal Flower Cave is a unique experience worth trying out because of its breathtaking coastline views and natural pools.

These are just a few examples of the island adventures that Barbados offers. The island provides a wide variety of activities and places to explore, whether you are interested in nature, history, or cultural experiences. So travel away from the shore and see everything Barbados has to offer.

- ***Day Trips to Other Island***

In addition to a multitude of sights and activities, Barbados is well situated within the Caribbean, making daily visits to neighboring islands possible. These outings provide you with the chance to discover other cultures, environments, and experiences. The following list of well-liked day tours from Barbados to other islands:

1. Grenadines: A magnificent archipelago of more than 30 islands and cays, the Grenadines are a well-liked day trip option from Barbados. You may visit islands like Bequia, Mustique, and Tobago Cays via a gorgeous boat journey or brief flight. These islands provide a perfect tropical getaway with their clean beaches, clear seas, and peaceful ambiance.

2. St. Lucia: This lovely island, which is located northwest of Barbados, is well known for its striking topography and unspoiled beauty. The famed Pitons, two volcanic peaks that majestically rise from the ocean, and Sulphur Springs, the only drive-through volcano in the world, are frequent stops on day excursions to St. Lucia. In addition, you may go zip-lining and snorkeling in the lovely hamlet of Soufrière.

3. Martinique: A French overseas territory with a distinctive fusion of Caribbean and European traditions, Martinique is a short flight from Barbados. The island has breathtaking beaches, a busy market, and a rich history. Discover Fort-de-France, the island's capital, go to Mount Pelée, or just savor the French-influenced food and shopping available there.

4. St. Vincent: The biggest island in the Grenadines, St. Vincent is situated west of Barbados. St. Vincent provides a rougher and more untamed natural scenery while being well-known for its beautiful rainforests, waterfalls, and black-sand beaches. Visit the Dark View Falls, the La Soufrière volcano, or the quiet beaches on a day excursion.

5. Dominica: Dominica is a haven for outdoor lovers and is referred to as the "Nature Island" in the Caribbean. Day trips from Barbados to Dominica sometimes include excursions like trekking through tropical jungles, going to hot springs, and checking out the well-known Boiling Lake. Beautiful rivers, waterfalls, and thriving marine life are all found on the island.

6. Antigua: This island nation, which sits northeast of Barbados, is renowned for its stunning white-sand beaches, interesting historical monuments, and vibrant culture. Visitors may explore destinations like Nelson's Dockyard, a UNESCO World Heritage Site, on day trips to Antigua, and take advantage of water sports like snorkeling, sailing, and swimming with stingrays at Stingray City.

It's crucial to research travel choices, such as planes or boat services, as well as any entrance restrictions or visa concerns while organizing a day excursion from Barbados to another island. To guarantee a smooth and pleasurable day trip, take into account the time required for travel and plan preparations appropriately.

- *Catamaran and Boat Tours*

Popular and entertaining methods to explore the stunning coastal waterways and marine life of Barbados are catamaran and boat trips. There are several catamaran and boat trips available to fit your interests, whether you're looking for a tranquil day at sea, snorkeling excursions, or sunset cruises. Here are a few of the adventures you can have:

1. Coastal Cruises: Board a catamaran or other vessel for a coastline tour of Barbados. The island's coastline, with its beautiful beaches, untamed cliffs, and picturesque coves, is often visible from these boats, offering breathtaking views. Enjoy the Caribbean Sea's magnificence while unwinding on the balcony and soaking up the sun.

2. Swimming and Snorkeling: Numerous catamaran trips in Barbados stop at great snorkeling locations. Visit the vivid coral reefs, swim with exotic creatures, and explore the fascinating underwater environment. A unique and unforgettable experience, swimming with sea turtles is also available on certain trips.

3. Underwater exploration: By taking a boat trip in a glass-bottomed boat or a semi-submarine, you may see the splendor of Barbados' underwater life without getting wet. These trips provide you with a wonderful look at the coral reefs and the rich marine life by letting you see through big windows into the underwater world.

4. Romantic Sunset Cruises: Spoil yourself with a sail around Barbados' coastline as the sun sets. Set sail in the late afternoon to take in the peaceful atmosphere and spectacular views of the sun setting over the Caribbean Sea. For an unforgettable evening, some sunset cruises may provide live music, beverages, and supper choices.

5. Private Charters: You may choose a private catamaran or boat charter for a more upscale experience. This enables you to personalize your schedule and take into account the tastes and interests of your party. exclusive charters provide a tailored and exclusive experience for any occasion, whether it is a family reunion, a celebration, or a business function.

6. Fishing Charters: You may go on a fishing trip to try your luck. Barbados is recognized for offering superb fishing chances. You will be taken to the ideal locations for capturing game fish including marlin, sailfish, and tuna by experts. The majority of the time, fishing charters give all the essential gear as well as the opportunity to pull in some outstanding specimens.

7. Party Cruises: If you want to have a vibrant and enjoyable experience, think about going on a party cruise. As you cruise around the coastline, these cruises often include music, dancing, and onboard entertainment. Make unforgettable experiences at a fun gathering with other tourists who share your interests.

When making reservations for catamaran and boat trips, it's crucial to choose reliable providers that place a priority on safety, have competent guides, and provide top-notch gear. Additionally, confirm if the trip includes extras like food, beverages, and snorkeling equipment as this varies depending on the particular tour. A catamaran or boat trip in Barbados is a great opportunity to appreciate the beauty of the Caribbean Sea and make lifelong memories, whether you're looking for adventure, leisure, or both.

- *Adventure Activities*

Barbados provides a variety of exhilarating adventure sports for people seeking an adrenaline rush thanks to its varied landscapes and warm Caribbean seas. Here are some thrilling adventure sports you may engage in Barbados, from the land to the sea:

1. Surfing: Barbados is a surfer's dream because of its constant Atlantic waves and lovely beaches. Go to the east coast, sometimes referred to as the "Soup Bowl," for world-class waves that are appropriate for both novice and expert surfers. For individuals wishing to learn or improve their talents, there are surf schools and rental establishments accessible.

2. Kiteboarding: Barbados is a great location for kiteboarding due to the island's consistent trade winds. On the south coast, go to Silver Rock Beach or Long Beach for good kiteboarding conditions and large open expanses. Both new riders and seasoned riders may take lessons and rent equipment.

3. Jet skiing: Take to Barbados' glistening seas on a jet ski you can rent. Experience the rush of speed as you travel the coastline, uncover secret coves, and even see marine life like flying fish and turtles. Popular beaches throughout the island provide jet ski rental options.

4. Ziplining: Fly through the trees on a zipline to get a bird's-eye perspective of Barbados' lush surroundings. For a thrilling zipline course that combines heart-pounding rides with breathtaking vistas, visit locations like Aerial Trek Zipline Adventure or Walkes Spring Plantation.

5. Off-Road Safari: Set off on an adventurous off-road safari journey to see Barbados' untamed interior. Embark on a 4x4 adventure across the island's lush woods, undiscovered routes, and stunning landscapes. This is a fantastic opportunity to see the island's natural beauty and explore its history, vegetation, and animals.

6. Cave Exploration: Barbados is well-known for its limestone caverns, and this adventurous activity provides a special opportunity to explore them. Take a tram excursion inside the magnificent limestone cave system known as Harrison's Cave to see its spectacular formations. Try spelunking with an experienced guide in the less-visited caverns for a more daring experience.

7. Deep-Sea Fishing: Take a thrilling deep-sea fishing expedition in the deep seas off Barbados. Try your hand at capturing game fish like marlin, tuna, and mahi-mahi by renting a boat. An effective and exciting fishing trip will be made possible by knowledgeable fishing guides who will provide the essential gear and impart their expertise.

Prioritizing safety is crucial while engaging in adventure activities. Be sure to use the proper safety equipment, heed the advice of skilled specialists, and be aware of your skill level and physical limitations.

Barbados provides a variety of adventure activities that are suitable for all levels of expertise, whether you're an adrenaline junkie or just want to spice up your holiday. Prepare to challenge your limits, enjoy the rush, and make priceless memories on this stunning Caribbean island.

IX. PRACTICAL INFORMATION

Money and Currency Issues

To have a seamless financial experience when visiting Barbados, it's crucial to get acquainted with the local money system and currencies. Here is some information about Barbados's MONEY and banking:

- **Currency:** The Barbadian dollar (BBD) is the national coinage of Barbados. The word "$" or "BDS$" stands for the currency. One US dollar is equivalent to two Barbadian dollars thanks to a 2:1 fixed exchange rate between the two currencies.

- **Currency Exchange:** Banks, authorized currency exchange offices, and the Grantley Adams International Airport all provide currency exchange services. When arriving, it's a good idea to convert a little of your native money for Barbados dollars to cover any urgent needs. Although most hotels, restaurants, and stores take major credit cards, it's always a good idea to have extra cash on hand for smaller businesses and neighborhood markets.

- **Automated Teller Machines (ATMs):** Automated Teller Machines (ATMs) are widely accessible in Barbados and the majority of them accept debit and credit cards from other countries. Banks, retail establishments, and famous tourist destinations all have ATMs. It is advised to let your bank know about your trip plans to confirm that your cards will function overseas and to find out whether there will be any costs associated with foreign withdrawals.

- **Banking:** Banks in Barbados normally are open from 8:00 AM to 3:00 PM on Monday through Thursday and from 8:00 AM to 5:00 PM on Friday. On Saturdays, certain banks may have fewer hours. The Royal Bank of Canada, Republic Bank, and FirstCaribbean International Bank are all significant banks. Banks provide some services, including cash withdrawals, currency exchange, and help with traveler's checks.

- **Traveler's checks:** While previously a prominent method of payment, traveler's checks are now less often accepted. To find out whether local banks or financial institutions in Barbados accept or can exchange traveler's checks, it is advisable to contact them directly. Transactions are often easier using credit and debit cards.

- **Tipping:** Tipping is customary in Barbados in exchange for courteous treatment. If a service fee has not already been applied, it is usual to leave a tip of 10% to 15% of the total bill at restaurants. Taxi drivers, tour guides, and hotel personnel all welcome gratuities for their services. Keeping a little cash on hand for tips is a smart idea.

- **Safety**: It's crucial to exercise care and pay attention to your possessions and personal safety while visiting any new place. Use a money belt or a covert wallet to carry your cash to keep it safe. Additionally, it's a good idea to create duplicates of crucial papers, like your passport, and store them apart from the originals in case of theft or loss.

You may have a trouble-free financial experience when traveling if you are acquainted with the local currency, banking options, and financial issues in Barbados. Enjoy your vacation in Barbados while making sensible and safe financial decisions.

Health and Safety Tips

To guarantee a hassle-free and pleasurable vacation to Barbados, it's crucial to put your health and safety first. Here are some recommendations for your visit's health and security:

1. Travel insurance: It is strongly advised to get travel insurance before leaving for Barbados to be covered for medical costs, trip cancellation or interruption, and emergency medical evacuation. Make sure the insurance coverage covers both the activities you want to participate in and any potential existing medical issues.

2. Vaccination: Find out whether any vaccines or preventative medicines are advised for Barbados by seeing your doctor or a travel clinic well before your trip. Routine immunizations, hepatitis A and B, typhoid, and tetanus-diphtheria vaccines are examples of common vaccines to think about.

3. Sun Protection: Because Barbados has a bright environment, it's important to shield oneself from the sun's potentially dangerous rays. The hottest period of the day is often between 10 am and 4 pm. Use sunscreen with a high SPF, wear a hat and sunglasses, and seek shade during this time.

4. Hydration: Keep yourself hydrated by drinking plenty of water, particularly in Barbados' warm heat. If you're doing outside activities or spending time in the sun, have a reusable water bottle with you and refill it often.

5. Food and Water Safety: To keep safe, always drink bottled water or water that has been properly treated and filtered. Do not consume tap water, ice, or beverages prepared with it. When purchasing street food, use caution and make sure it is hot and freshly prepared. Use hand sanitizer or often wash your hands before eating.

6. Mosquito Protection: Use DEET-containing insect repellent, wear long sleeves and long trousers, and stay in accommodations with screens or air conditioning to guard against mosquito-borne diseases including dengue, Zika, and chikungunya. If you're staying in more remote places, you may want to think about utilizing bed nets.

7. General Safety Precautions: Follow these when touring Barbados. Keep an eye on your possessions and keep pricey goods hidden. Utilize trustworthy cab services and avoid using unlicensed taxis. When swimming in the ocean, use caution and heed any safety flags or warnings posted on the beaches.

8. Emergency Contact Information: Become familiar with the local emergency telephone numbers in Barbados. For non-life-threatening emergencies, dial 211; for life-threatening ones, dial 511. In case of crises or unforeseen circumstances, have a list of crucial phone numbers handy, including the number for your embassy or consulate.

9. COVID-19 Precautions: Keep up with the most recent COVID-19-related travel warnings and health recommendations. Follow local laws, use face masks in public if necessary, maintain a physical distance, and follow any further instructions issued by Barbadian authorities.

Before any trip, it's always a good idea to speak with a healthcare provider or travel clinic to get individualized recommendations based on your medical history and unique travel arrangements.

You may reduce hazards, keep well, and have a memorable and pleasurable experience touring Barbados by heeding these health and safety recommendations.

Communication and Internet

While visiting Barbados, being connected and having dependable communication options are crucial for a hassle-free and pleasurable vacation. The following details pertain to internet and communication services in Barbados:

1. Mobile Network Coverage: Broad coverage over the whole island is provided by Barbados' well-developed mobile network infrastructure. Digicel and Flow are the two main mobile network carriers in Barbados. Prepaid SIM cards are readily available from both providers and may be bought and activated for usage in GSM-compatible phones that have been unlocked.

2. SIM Cards and Mobile Plans: Purchasing a regional SIM card might be a reasonably priced way to remain connected while visiting Barbados. SIM cards are sold in a variety of retail locations, including grocery stores, convenience stores, and shops for mobile network providers. You may choose from phone calls, text messages, and data choices with prepaid plans, enabling you to control your spending and use.

3. Roaming: If you want to utilize your home cell network while visiting Barbados, ask your service provider about the alternatives and charges for international roaming. Before using your phone while traveling, it's crucial to understand the tariffs and any data restrictions since roaming fees may be pricey.

4. Wi-Fi: There is a lot of Wi-Fi in Barbados, especially at hotels, resorts, eateries, and coffee shops. Many businesses provide their patrons with free Wi-Fi connections. Furthermore, certain public spaces, like parks and retail malls, could provide free Wi-Fi connections. Remember that Wi-Fi connection quality and speed might vary, particularly in more rural regions.

5. Internet Cafes: Though they are less common than they once were, you may still find a handful in Barbados, especially in tourist hotspots. If you don't have your device or need a dependable connection, these cafés provide computer stations with internet access for a cost.

6. Voice over IP (VoIP) and Messaging Applications: Using VoIP and messaging applications like WhatsApp, Facebook Messenger, or Skype may be a practical and affordable method to remain in contact with loved ones while visiting Barbados. Instead of using voice calls or regular SMS, these applications use internet data, which may reduce communication costs.

7. Emergency Services: To contact local emergency services in an emergency, call 511 in an emergency or 211 in a non-life-threatening crisis. Note down these numbers as well as any other crucial contacts, such as the ones for your embassy or consulate.

Before your journey to Barbados, confirm the international coverage, roaming capabilities, and related expenses with your cell service provider. During your travel to Barbados, making use of local SIM cards, Wi-Fi hotspots, and online messaging applications may help you remain connected and control communication costs.

Useful Phrases and Local Etiquette

When visiting Barbados, it's usually beneficial to get acquainted with certain practical sayings and regional etiquette to improve relationships with locals and demonstrate respect for the local way of life. Here are some important words to remember and some etiquette advice:

Useful Phrases:
1. Hello - "Good morning" (used until midday) or "Good afternoon"

2. Thank you - "Thank you" or "Thanks"
3. Please - "Please" or "Pardon me"
4. Excuse me - "Excuse me" or "Sorry"
5. Yes
6. No
7. Do you speak English?
8. How much does it cost?
9. Where is...?
10. Goodbye - "Goodbye" or "See you later"

Local Etiquette:

1. Greetings: Barbadians are often kind and courteous. When you enter a store, or restaurant, or are meeting someone for the first time, smile and say "Good morning" or "Good afternoon" to them.

2. Courtesy: Use the words "please" and "thank you" while speaking with natives. Barbados places a strong importance on politeness, thus being respectful will be welcomed.

3. Dress Code: Barbados has a rather formal dress code, particularly for more formal occasions. It is advised to dress modestly and refrain from wearing beachwear or exposing attire while visiting churches, government institutions, or luxury restaurants.

4. Punctuality: It's polite to appear on time for planned appointments, meetings, or excursions since Barbadians in general value punctuality.

5. Table Manners: When eating out, be considerate to others and wait to be seated. Wait until everyone has been served before beginning your meal, and keep your elbows away from the table while doing so. A modest tip is also often left for excellent service unless one is already included in the bill.

6. Public Behavior: Act politely while in public. Be sensitive to other people's personal space and refrain from noisy or disruptive conduct.

7. Tipping: In Barbados, tipping is traditional. If a service fee hasn't already been applied, it's customary to leave a tip of 10% to 15% of the entire bill at restaurants. For services like taxi rides, hotel employees, and tour guides, tips are also very appreciated.

8. Respect for Environment: Barbados is proud of its natural beauty. By properly disposing of waste and observing designated conservation zones, you may aid in environmental preservation. While participating in aquatic activities, take care not to harm coral reefs and other marine ecosystems.

9. Cultural Respect: Barbados has a rich cultural history. Respect the regional traditions, customs, and historical landmarks. Before shooting pictures of people or holy places, get their permission.

10. Language: Barbados' official language is English. Even though some residents speak the

Bajan dialect, English is generally understood and used across the whole island.

You'll have a more pleasurable and culturally engaging experience when visiting Barbados if you apply these helpful sayings and observe local protocol. Always keep in mind that developing relationships and cultivating fruitful encounters with locals begins with having a polite attitude.

Navigating the Island

Due to its small size and well-kept road network, Barbados is a very simple island to navigate. Here are a few pointers for getting about the island:

1. Maps and GPS: Use a GPS navigation device or have a map of Barbados handy before you go. There are many places to find maps, including hotels, visitor information centers, and internet mapping services. Turn-by-turn instructions may also be found in GPS navigation applications for smartphones.

2. Road Signs: Pay close attention to the road signs since they provide crucial information including cautions, speed restrictions, and instructions. The majority of the traffic signs in Barbados adhere to international standards, therefore foreign drivers ought to be able to recognize them.

3. Landmarks and Points of Reference: Barbados is home to several significant landmarks and points of comparison that may be used for navigation. A few examples of these landmarks include roundabouts, churches, schools, and eminent structures. It might be useful to use these landmarks as guides, particularly while traveling through smaller towns or rural regions without many street signs.

4. Bridgetown Reference Point: When traversing the island, Bridgetown, Barbados' capital city, is often utilized as the main reference point. Some several significant highways and roads go to or pass through Bridgetown. You might think about utilizing Bridgetown as a beginning or finishing point for your journeys.

5. Road Conditions: Barbados' roads are typically in good condition, particularly in the more populous regions. Drive carefully and obey speed restrictions, since some rural or less-traveled roads may have fewer lanes or uneven terrain. When it rains heavily, drive with particular care since the roadways may turn slick.

6. Traffic Congestion: Busier neighborhoods like Bridgetown and famous tourist routes may have traffic congestion during peak hours. Plan your trips appropriately, leaving additional time in case there are any delays. If you can, try to avoid busy hours or take other routes to avoid congested areas.

7. Public Transportation: If you'd rather not drive, Barbados offers choices like buses and taxis for public transit. Public buses may be an affordable way to travel and cover the majority of the island. Also easily accessible and capable of offering quick door-to-door service are taxis.

8. Asking for Directions: Don't be afraid to ask the locals for help or instructions if you need them. Barbadians may provide you with advice or correctly lead you, and they are often kind and helpful.

Keep in mind to educate yourself about local traffic laws and drive according to them, especially staying to the left of the road. As you visit Barbados, pay attention to your surroundings and take in the island's breathtaking scenery. Barbados should be manageable and delightful to navigate with some planning and preparation.

X. SHOPPING AND SOUVENIRS

Barbados provides a range of shopping options, from sophisticated shops to regional markets. Here is a list of places to buy and find mementos on the island:

- *Popular Shopping Areas*

From neighborhood markets to posh retail areas, Barbados provides a wide variety of shopping opportunities. Here are a few of the island's well-liked retail areas:

1. Bridgetown: Bridgetown, the capital of Barbados, is a thriving center for shopping. Bridgetown's Broad Street and Swan Street are well-known shopping areas featuring a variety of regional retailers, global brands, department stores, and duty-free shops.

2. Holetown: Holetown is another well-liked shopping location and is situated on the west coast of Barbados. A prestigious shopping center in Holetown, The Limegrove Lifestyle Centre is home to exclusive boutiques, high-end retailers, jewelry stores, galleries, and eateries.

3. St. Lawrence Gap: Located on the south coast, St. Lawrence Gap provides a diverse selection of restaurants, shopping, and nightlife. There are several shops along "The Gap" that offer apparel, swimsuits, trinkets, and regional crafts. It's a bustling neighborhood with a terrific vibe for entertainment and shopping.

4. Pelican Village: Located in Bridgetown, Pelican Village is a cultural hub and marketplace where regional artists may display their skills. It has several bright chattel homes where you can discover a variety of regionally produced crafts, including ceramics, wood sculptures, fabrics, and jewelry.

5. Sheraton Mall: The Sheraton Mall, a sizable shopping complex with a mix of domestic and foreign merchants, is situated in Christ Church. There are several shops there that sell apparel, accessories, gadgets, household products, and other items. A grocery and food court are also included in the mall.

6. Oistins Fish Market: In addition to being well known for its fresh fish, Oistins Fish

Market is a terrific location to buy handcrafted goods and trinkets from the area. The Oistins Fish Fry brings the neighborhood to life on Friday evenings with live music, food booths, and artisan merchants.

7. Chattel Village: In Holetown, Chattel Village is a group of vibrant chattel cottages that have been turned into stores. Here, you may explore a variety of shops that sell handmade goods, original artwork, apparel, and accessories from the area. It is a quaint and beautiful retail district.

8. Cheapside Market: Head to Bridgetown's Cheapside Market for a taste of a local market. This lively market is a hive of activity for local cuisine, fresh fruit, spices, and crafts. It's a fantastic location for discovering distinctive goods and getting a taste of the local culture.

Check the operating hours before visiting these retail places since they may change. Remember that many shops in Barbados can be closed on Sundays and national holidays as well.

Barbados has a variety of shopping districts to suit all tastes and price ranges, whether you're seeking high-end goods, regional crafts, or fresh fruit. Discover local treasures and souvenirs while taking advantage of the unique shopping opportunities the island has to offer.

- *Local Products and Crafts*

Barbados is renowned for having a thriving arts and crafts industry that offers a wide range of regional goods that showcase the creativity and culture of the island. When traveling to Barbados, be sure to look out for the following popular local goods and crafts:

1. Pottery: A treasured art form that highlights the island's creative prowess is Barbadian pottery. Find products made of pottery that are handcrafted, such as bowls, vases, plates, and ornamental items. You may get exquisitely created ceramic items at the famous pottery company Earthworks Pottery in St. Thomas.

2. Basketry: Straw crafts and woven baskets are essential to Barbadian culture. These baskets, which come in a variety of sizes and forms, are made locally from materials like sisal and palm leaves. They are ideal for keeping fruits, bread, or other household things, and they make for beautiful and useful keepsakes.

3. Batik and tie-dye: Fabrics made with colorful batik and tie-dye patterns have a long history in Barbados. Look for items with these vibrant and distinctive patterns on apparel, scarves, purses, and accessories. These unique, eye-catching keepsakes are crafted from handwoven fabrics.

4. Jewelry made from shells and coral: Barbados is home to stunning seashells and coral reefs, and local jewelers often include these organic components in their creations. Look for jewelry created from shells, coral, and sea glass, such as earrings, necklaces, bracelets, and other accessories. These jewelry souvenirs are distinctive and beautifully depict the spirit of the island.

5. Local Artworks: Barbados has a booming art scene, and you can discover a variety of works that capture the beauty and culture of the island. Look for local artists' paintings, prints, sculptures, and mixed-media works of art. Explore artisan markets and art galleries to find one-of-a-kind items that embody the character of Barbados.

6. Rum and Rum-related Product: Barbados is well known for its rum manufacturing. Bring a bottle of Barbadian rum home as a tasty keepsake. Additionally, rum-related goods that highlight the island's rum legacy include rum cakes, rum-infused chocolates, rum punch mixes, and other rum-related items.

7. Hot Sauce and Seasonings: Barbados is renowned for its rich and hot food. Find a range of spicy sauces, pepper jellies, and seasonings created using regional peppers and spices by browsing local food markets and specialized stores. These seasonings give your meals a fiery boost and make wonderful presents.

8. Herbal Products: Barbados has a long history of using herbs, and there are many herbal products available that are manufactured from local herbs and components. Try to find natural products that include traditional medicinal herbs like neem, aloe vera, and lemongrass in your drinks, lotions, and oils.

9. Supporting Regional Artists and Vendors: Consider supporting regional artists and shopping from reliable vendors when you purchase goods and crafts made in your area. To assure authenticity, look for products that have been handcrafted in Barbados or have the "Made in Barbados" logo.

Discovering the regional goods and crafts of Barbados enables you to interact with the people, customs, and talented craftspeople of the island. These one-of-a-kind keepsakes not only remember you of your trip, but they also help the community's economy and support the preservation of Barbadian workmanship.

XI. FAMILIES IN BARBADOS

With a variety of activities and attractions suitable for all ages, Barbados is a fantastic vacation spot for families. Here is a guide to having a family-friendly time in Barbados:

1. Beaches: Barbados is well known for its stunning beaches, which provide many chances for family entertainment. Visit well-known family-friendly beaches including Carlisle Bay, Accra Beach, and Mullins Beach to go swimming, making sandcastles, snorkeling, and participating in other water activities.

2. Wildlife Encounters: Go on an expedition with your family to discover the diverse fauna of the island. Visit the Barbados Wildlife Reserve to see local wildlife in its natural habitat, including green monkeys, tortoises, and exotic birds. On the northern shore, you may also visit the Animal Flower Cave to see the aquatic life that resides in its pools.

3. Glass-Bottom Boat and Submarine Tours: See the undersea world without getting wet! Take your family on a glass-bottom boat trip or a submarine cruise to see the colorful fish, coral reefs, and other aquatic life that call the beautiful waters around Barbados home.

4. Family-Friendly Attractions: Barbados has several family-friendly attractions. Discover the rich history and culture of the island by visiting the Barbados Museum and Historical Society. Visit the UNESCO-listed Barbados Garrison Historical Area or the Barbados Wildlife Reserve, both of which have historic structures and military relics.

5. Adventure Parks: Take part in some exhilarating activities at adventure parks like Barbados Zip Line and Aerial Trekking Tour or Atlantis Submarines Underwater Adventures. These amusement parks provide thrilling opportunities for both children and adults, letting you soar over the trees or delve deep into the water.

6. Water Parks: Visit the neighborhood water parks to unwind and have a splashing good time. All ages may enjoy the slides, pools, and water play areas at Bridgetown's well-liked Pirate's Cove Water Park. It's a terrific spot to enjoy a day of family-friendly activities.

7. Catamaran Cruises: Board a catamaran for a leisurely trip around the island while snorkeling and swimming with sea turtles. A lot of catamaran trips are designed exclusively for families, making sure that everyone on board has a fun and safe time.

8. Kids' Clubs and Childcare Services: Many resorts in Barbados have kids' clubs and childcare services if you're searching for some adult time or want help with childcare. Parents may rest and unwind while their kids are entertained and engaged in supervised activities at these clubs.

9. Cultural Experiences: Take your family to cultural events like the Crop Over Festival or the Oistins Fish Festival to fully immerse them in Barbados' rich culture. These festivals provide a pleasant and instructive experience for the entire family by showcasing local music, dancing, and food.

10. Accommodation Options: A variety of family-friendly lodging choices are available in Barbados, including resorts, hotels, and rental homes. To guarantee a relaxing and pleasurable visit, look for accommodations with features like kid-friendly pools, play spaces, and planned kids' activities.

Families may go to Barbados where there are a variety of fun activities and attractions to keep everyone engaged. Your family will undoubtedly make lifelong memories in this tropical paradise, from taking advantage of the beaches and animal encounters to learning about the island's history and cultural activities.

- *Travel Tips for Family*

A few pointers will assist you and your family have a smooth and pleasurable journey while visiting Barbados. Here are some suggestions for family travelers to Barbados:

1. Plan Ahead: To make the most of your stay in Barbados, research and organize your activities in advance. Make an agenda that incorporates a variety of family-friendly sights and activities by taking into account the interests and preferences of each family member.

2. Pack Accordingly: Include necessities for the whole family, like sunscreen, caps, swimsuits, and comfy clothes. Bring any essential prescriptions, infant supplies, and children's entertainment materials like books, toys, or technological gadgets.

3. Stay Hydrated: Due to Barbados' potential for heat, it's crucial to drink enough water, particularly while spending time outside. Bring water bottles for the whole family and sip on them often during the day.

4. Beach Safety: Barbados has some stunning beaches, but beach safety should always come first, particularly if you're with kids. Follow lifeguard instructions, keep an eye out for any beach warnings or currents, and always keep an eye on your kids. To protect yourself from the sun's rays, don't forget to often reapply sunscreen.

5. Embrace Local Cuisine: With Barbados' wide culinary scene, it's a wonderful chance to expose your kids to different tastes and cuisine. Encourage them to sample some of the regional Bajan dishes, such as flying fish, cou-cou, and macaroni pie. There are kid-friendly alternatives available at many eateries, so there is something for every palate.

6. Transportation: Think about the best solutions for your family's transportation needs. When you hire a vehicle, you have more freedom, particularly if you want to go about the island. As an alternative, cabs and public transit are widely accessible and might be a practical and economical choice.

7. Safety Precautions: Know the whereabouts of the closest medical facilities and emergency phone numbers. Additionally, it's a good idea to pack a basic first aid package in case you get any small illnesses or injuries while traveling.

8. Family-Friendly Accommodation: Opt for lodging options that have features like kid-friendly pools, playgrounds, or kids' clubs. Families may stay in the many resorts and hotels in Barbados with the assurance of a pleasant and pleasurable vacation for everybody.

9. Respect Local Customs: Inform your kids about Barbados' regional traditions and cultural values. Encourage children to respect the community, observe clothing requirements while visiting religious sites, and use caution when acting in public.

10. Enjoy Family Time: Keep in mind to take some time to unwind and cherish special family occasions. There are many chances for beach picnics, wildlife hikes, and entertaining activities in Barbados. Enjoy your time together to the fullest and make enduring memories.

You may have a pleasant and pleasurable family trip in Barbados by heeding this travel advice. Explore and make fantastic family memories as you embrace the island's beauty, culture, and welcoming hospitality.

XII. EVENTS AND FESTIVALS

Barbados is renowned for hosting exciting festivals and events all year round. These events highlight the island's diverse customs, music, cuisine, and culture. The following are some of the most popular celebrations and events in Barbados that you may like attending:

- *Crop Over Festival*

Barbados' lively and joyous Crop Over festival marks the conclusion of the sugarcane harvest season. It is one of the most eagerly awaited and well-attended events on the island, drawing both residents and tourists. Typically beginning in June and ending with the Grand Kadooment Day procession in early August, Crop Over lasts for several weeks. An outline of the many Crop Over customs and activities is provided below:

1. Ceremonial Opening: The event begins with a ceremonial opening that often includes the symbolic delivery of the final sugarcane to signal the conclusion of the harvest season.

2. Calypso and Soca Competition: Crop Over is renowned for its exciting contests for Calypso and Soca Music. On these occasions, local musicians display their skills and originality while writing songs that capture the festival's mood and relevant social and political topics.

The contests create anticipation and establish the musical ambiance of the festival.

3. Cohobblopot: During Crop Over, Cohobblopot is a greatly awaited event. Top artists from both domestic and other countries will play at this massive performance. Live performances during the event feature the upbeat and contagious rhythms of calypso and soca music, keeping the audience dancing all night long.

4. Pic-O-De-Crop Finals: The Pic-O-De-Crop Finals, the championship of the calypso competition, is one of Crop Over's highlights. The finalists provide compelling and exciting performances that address social, cultural, and political concerns as they fight for the esteemed title of Calypso Monarch.

5. Bridgetown Market: During Crop Over, Bridgetown, the nation's capital, hosts a crowded street market known as Bridgetown Market. It has a huge selection of vendors offering regional crafts, apparel, food, and drinks. Traditional Bajan cuisine may be sampled by guests, who can also take in the colorful environment and live entertainment.

6. Crop Over Heritage Walk: Visitors are taken on a guided tour of Crop Over's past and present. It examines the festival's importance, historical development, and accompanying cultural customs.

7. Grand Kadooment Day: The much-anticipated Grand Kadooment Day procession serves as Crop Over's big conclusion. Participants dress in colorful, ornate costumes that portray a variety of themes and dance around Bridgetown to the upbeat calypso and soca beats. In the National Stadium, where the procession ends, contestants are assessed on their performances and costumes.

Crop Over honors Barbados' extensive cultural legacy in addition to celebrating music and dancing. The event displays the island's skill, inventiveness, and sense of camaraderie. It offers the chance to fully experience the contagious spirit and bright environment of Bajan culture, making it an unforgettable and thrilling event for everyone who takes part.

- *Reggae Festival*

Every year, the Barbados Reggae Festival honors the deep and energetic sounds of reggae music. For a series of performances and activities spread out around the island, the festival brings together regional and worldwide reggae performers. An outline of the Barbados Reggae Festival is provided below:

1. Concerts: Renowned reggae musicians will play during the event in a variety of Barbados locations. Reggae fans may enjoy a variety of musical genres within the genre, including roots reggae, dancehall, and current reggae, at small inside shows as well as massive outdoor events.

2. Beach Parties: The beach parties are one of the highlights of the Barbados Reggae Festival. These exciting activities take place on the island's stunning beaches, fostering a joyful and laid-back attitude. Participants may take in the sand, water, and colorful beach culture while grooving to the beat of reggae music.

3. Themed Events: The festival often has themed events that highlight various facets of Caribbean culture and reggae music. These occasions could include concerts paying homage to legendary reggae artists, DJ showcases, sound system fights and cultural exhibits showcasing the impact of reggae on diverse art forms.

4. After Parties: At nearby clubs and venues, after parties are hosted while the festivities continue late into the evening. These gatherings provide a chance to meet with other music fans while dancing to reggae sounds in a fun and vivacious setting.

5. Workshops & Seminars: The festival sometimes includes instructive sessions that explore the background, cultural relevance, and development of reggae music. These discussions might include subjects like how reggae has influenced social and political movements or how Jamaican music has influenced music throughout the world.

Both locals and tourists from across the globe who are enthusiastic about reggae music and Caribbean culture go to the Barbados Reggae Festival. It provides a stage for both seasoned and up-and-coming reggae performers to display their talents and engage with a wide audience. Reggae music's contagious rhythms, upbeat energy, and inspirational messages may be experienced at the event, giving attendees an amazing experience.

- *Oistins Fish Festival*

In the coastal Barbados village of Oistins, there is a well-known cultural celebration called the

Oistins Fish Festival. It honors the island's fishing past and provides both residents and tourists with a distinctive and exciting experience. The Oistins Fish Festival will include the following, in general:

1. Seafood Delights: The festival's main focus is on highlighting the wealth of fresh seafood that Barbados has to offer. Fish, fish cakes, shrimp, lobster, and other delectable seafood meals are served from grills and booths put up by local fishermen and traders. It's a chance to enjoy scrumptious seafood delicacies and the tastes of Bajan cuisine.

2. Fisherman's Parade: A vibrant and energetic Fisherman's Parade ushers in the event. Local fisherman parade through the streets of Oistins while displaying their boats and fishing equipment with pride. It is a colorful event that highlights the significance of fishing to Barbadian culture.

3. Entertainment and Music: Entertainment and Music are well-known features of the Oistins Fish Festival. Local bands and artists enter the stage and present a variety of Caribbean music, including calypso, reggae, soca, and other styles. Visitors are invited to participate in the dancing and festivities because of the contagious rhythms and exciting presentations.

4. Cultural Performances: Additional cultural shows that reflect different facets of Barbadian culture are included in the festival. Traditional folk music, dance performances, and cultural exhibits that highlight the island's history and customs are available for your enjoyment.

5. Arts & Crafts: You may check out regional arts and crafts during the Oistins Fish Festival. To provide customers the chance to take home a bit of Barbadian culture and creativity, vendors put up booths offering handcrafted goods including jewelry, paintings, ceramics, and other crafts.

6. Sporting Events: The festival often includes sporting events that encourage teamwork and friendly rivalry. Beach volleyball, cricket tournaments, and other sporting activities are available for visitors to take part in, or they may just watch the action.

7. Family-Friendly Environment: The Oistins Fish Festival is renowned for its welcoming atmosphere. It's a fantastic excursion for families to enjoy together since there are entertainment choices and activities appropriate for all ages.

The Oistins Fish Festival showcases Barbados' illustrious fishing tradition with a distinctive fusion of culinary delicacies, cultural exhibits, and festive festivities. It's a fantastic chance to get immersed in the community's culture, gorge on delectable seafood, and encounter the kind hospitality of the Barbadian people.

XIII. BEYOND TOURISM

Barbados is a lively, dynamic island that provides many prospects for growth and development in other industries apart from tourism. Beyond tourism, Barbados has been concentrating its efforts on the following areas:

1. Financial Services: Barbados has been putting effort into bolstering its standing as a recognized worldwide financial services hub. The island provides a variety of financial and investment services, including wealth management, offshore banking, and insurance. There have been initiatives to strengthen the legal system, draw in outside capital, and foster innovation in the industry.

2. Innovation and Information Technology: Barbados has been making investments to grow its industry of innovation and information technology. To aid startups and business owners, the island has built technological parks and incubators. The objective is to promote innovation, draw in tech talent, and promote the expansion of digital companies and services.

3. Renewable Energy: Barbados has made great progress in implementing renewable energy sources and lowering its reliance on fossil fuels. The construction of solar farms and the installation of solar panels on public buildings are only two of the efforts that the island has put into place to encourage solar energy. Barbados wants to lead the Caribbean region in renewable energy and set an example for sustainable development.

4. Education and Research: Education and research are highly valued in Barbados. There are several colleges and educational institutes on the island that provide a variety of programs. To promote economic development and diversity, efforts have been undertaken to establish research partnerships, support educational innovation, and build a competent workforce.

5. Agriculture and Agro-Processing: Barbados has been making investments to resurrect its agricultural industry and promote agro-processing. The island wants to increase food security, support environmentally friendly agricultural methods, and create value-added goods from locally produced food. Initiatives like aquaponics, organic farming, and agrotourism have gained popularity recently.

6. Cultural Industries: Barbados is aware of the economic potential of its thriving cultural sectors, which include the arts, music, fashion, and cinema. To encourage international connections and collaborations, build creative clusters, and support and promote local talent, efforts have been undertaken. The island's rich cultural past is a priceless asset that supports its growth on the social and economic fronts.

7. Health and Wellness: Barbados has been promoting itself as a location for wellness and health tourism. Numerous holistic health facilities, spa resorts, and wellness retreats with an emphasis on relaxation are available on the island. Barbados also aims to grow its medical tourism industry by offering top-notch medical facilities and services.

Barbados is dedicated to expanding its economy beyond tourism and creating a sustainable future. The island hopes to generate new possibilities, attract investment, and foster talent and innovation by concentrating on these areas of growth. This all-encompassing strategy guarantees Barbados' long-term development and prosperity while conserving its distinctive cultural and natural assets.

- *Volunteering Opportunities*

If you want to help out your community and support charitable organizations, Barbados has some volunteer options available. You might look at the following volunteer opportunities in Barbados:

1. Community Development: Community development projects, such as enhancing access to social services, healthcare, and education, are a major emphasis of many organizations in Barbados. You may volunteer with nearby NGOs and community organizations to help with initiatives that benefit underserved populations, mentor young people, or work with community outreach programs.

2. Environmental Protection: Barbados is renowned for having varied ecosystems and stunning natural scenery. By taking part in tree-planting campaigns, animal conservation programs, and beach clean-ups, you can support environmental conservation efforts. Opportunities to support environmental preservation are provided by groups like the Barbados Sea Turtle Project and the Barbados National Trust.

3. Animal Welfare: If you have a strong interest in animal welfare, you may volunteer in Barbados at wildlife sanctuaries, rescue facilities, or animal shelters. To support their animal care, rehabilitation, and educational initiatives, these organizations often depend on volunteers. Working with rescued animals, contributing to conservation initiatives, or taking part in awareness campaigns might all be opportunities for you.

4. Education and Youth Development: Education and youth empowerment are very important in Barbados. Volunteering is a great way to promote educational projects, provide tutoring or mentorship, plan workshops or recreational events for kids and teens, and engage with after-school programs, youth groups, and schools. It's a chance to make a difference in the lives of kids and support their academic and personal development.

5. Health and Social Services: You may help vulnerable populations and work to improve the well-being of those in need by volunteering for healthcare or social service organizations. You may help out at healthcare facilities like hospitals, clinics, or groups that serve individuals with impairments or long-term diseases or those who need mental health care.

6. Sports and Recreation: Barbados has a thriving sports culture, and helping out with sports initiatives may be satisfying. You may become engaged in sports projects that encourage physical exercise, collaboration, and personal growth by coaching, planning sporting events, or supporting them.

It's crucial to do your homework and get in touch with trustworthy groups that share your interests and beliefs if you're thinking about volunteering in Barbados. To learn more about possibilities and the particular criteria for volunteering, get in touch with regional non-governmental organizations (NGOs), community centers, or international volunteer groups that are active in Barbados. When you volunteer in Barbados, you can interact with the local population, learn about the culture, and make a real impact while taking advantage of the island's friendliness and hospitality.

- *Local Community Engagement*

While traveling to Barbados, getting involved in the community might lead to a richer and more fulfilling experience. During your stay, you may interact with the neighborhood in the following ways:

1. Attend Cultural Events and Festivals: Barbados is renowned for its lively festivals and cultural events. Take part in festivals like Crop Over, Holetown Festival, or Oistins Fish Festival to get a taste of the customs, music, dancing, and gastronomic delicacies of the area. These gatherings are a wonderful chance to meet people and learn more about their traditions and history.

2. Support Local Businesses: To enjoy genuine Bajan cuisine and help the community's economy, choose to eat at neighborhood cafés, restaurants, and food stands. To buy goods, souvenirs, and handicrafts manufactured locally, visit markets, craft stores, and boutiques. Supporting regional companies directly supports

Barbadians' way of life and encourages environmentally friendly travel strategies.

3. Participate in Community-based Tourism: Look for community-based tourism programs that let you interact with local people and discover their way of life. Activities like village tours, homestays, or cultural exchanges might fall under this category. Participating in these activities encourages meaningful connections, advances intercultural understanding, and has positive economic effects on the neighborhood.

4. Volunteer with Local Organizations: Take into account lending your time and expertise to neighborhood nonprofits or community initiatives. You may support campaigns that promote social services, healthcare, environmental protection, or education. By getting your hands dirty, you may contribute to the community, forge relationships with the people there, and learn more about their struggles and hopes.

5. Participate in Workshops and Classes: Enroll in seminars or programs that provide insights into the customs, skills, and culture of the area. Alongside local specialists, learn how to prepare Bajan delicacies, perform traditional music, or make crafts. These encounters give chances for cultural exchange and an opportunity to benefit from the local community's knowledge and experience.

6. Interact with Locals: While traveling, strike up talks with locals. Conversations with Barbadians may provide insightful information about their lives, viewpoints, and the way of life in the country, whether it is with a seller at a market, a tour guide, or a chance meeting at a café.

7. Respect Local Customs and Etiquette: To show respect for the culture of the island of Barbados, get to know the customs and etiquette there. Say "Good morning," "Good afternoon," or "Good evening" to folks when you enter a room. When visiting religious places or going to cultural events, be aware of the clothing requirement. Building a relationship with the locals may also be facilitated by learning a few fundamental words and phrases, such as "hello" and "thank you," in the language.

Getting involved with the local Barbados community not only enhances your trip experience, but also offers chances for cultural exchange, mutual understanding, and the development of good connections between tourists and residents. Accept the friendliness and generosity of the Barbadians, and go into your contacts with an open mind and a sincere desire to connect and learn.

- ***Giving Back to Barbados***

Giving back to Barbados is a fantastic way to express gratitude for the friendliness of the people and the natural beauty of the island. Here are some ideas on how you may help and have a good influence:

1. Volunteer for Local Charities and Non-Profit Organizations: Community development, education, environmental preservation, and social welfare are the main priorities of many local charities and nonprofits in Barbados. Look for chances to donate your time, talents, or resources to these organizations. You might lend a hand with fund-raising activities, help with neighborhood initiatives, or provide guidance and educational assistance to nearby people or organizations.

2. Support Neighborhood Schools and Educational Initiatives: One important area where you may have an impact is education. Think about giving books, school supplies, or instructional materials to the neighborhood schools. You might also look into student mentoring programs that provide direction and assistance, or you could offer your services as a guest speaker so that you can impart your wisdom.

3. Contribute to Environmental Conservation: Barbados is renowned for its stunning beaches, coral reefs, and unique ecosystems. Support regional environmental groups that prioritize preservation initiatives, beach clean-ups, and sustainable lifestyles. You may take part in volunteer programs or donate to initiatives that seek to preserve ecosystems, safeguard marine life, or encourage eco-friendly travel.

4. Donate to Local Causes: Donate to a local organization after doing some research to find one that fits your interests and beliefs. To help these charities, think about giving monetary or in-kind contributions. Your gift may have a significant influence on community development programs, animal welfare groups, or healthcare initiatives.

5. Engage in Responsible Tourism Practices: Respect the local community, environment, and culture while traveling responsibly. Select lodgings, tour companies, and other establishments that have an emphasis on sustainable practices and community involvement. This helps the local economy and guarantees that the effects of your trip will be favorable for the area.

6. Buy Locally Made Goods: By doing so, you may help out your neighborhood's artists, craftspeople, and business owners. This helps to conserve traditional crafts and cultural heritage in addition to boosting the local economy. Look for markets, artisan shows, or stores that sell genuine goods made in the area.

7. Share Your Experience: Let others know about Barbados' distinctive culture, breathtaking scenery, and kind welcome. Talk about your wonderful experiences with your loved ones and internet communities. Encourage sensible travel habits and emphasize the value of helping the neighborhood and protecting the island's resources.

Always keep in mind that helping Barbados means making an influence that will last. To make sure that your gifts are used properly and meet the needs of the local community, it is crucial to do your research and establish connections with recognized organizations and projects. By helping others, you contribute to Barbados' long-term growth and well-being, providing an enduring legacy for incoming tourists to enjoy.

XIV. FINAL THOUGHTS AND TRAVEL TIPS

Travelers may enjoy a wide variety of adventures on the alluring island of Barbados. The island has much to offer everyone, from its beautiful beaches and lush scenery to its rich culture and kind hospitality. Barbados provides everything you're looking for whether you want to unwind, go on an adventure, experience another culture, or do all of the above.

Remember to adopt sustainable travel habits, respect the culture, and interact with the locals while you visit the island. Be aware of the environment, purchase eco-friendly products, and assist local companies. You may contribute to conserving Barbados' natural beauty and boosting the regional economy by doing this.

Barbados is home to a wealth of attractions, from the energetic Bridgetown, the island's capital, to the quaint coastal settlements and historical landmarks. Discover the breathtaking beaches, savor delectable food, and take part in the island's lively festivals and cultural activities. Don't forget to travel beyond the popular tourist destinations and find the undiscovered treasures that highlight the island's natural beauty and historical legacy.

Barbados provides a wide range of experiences and activities to fit your interests, whether you're traveling with family, searching for adventure, or just trying to relax. There are plenty of experiences to go on, from hiking and discovering the island's natural marvels to water sports and diving.

Consider the ideal time to visit Barbados, visa requirements, travel alternatives, and other practical factors as you prepare for your trip. To guarantee a simple and delightful trip, do research and make advance plans.

Barbados will capture your heart and leave you with priceless memories; it's more than simply a location to go on holiday. So prepare to immerse yourself in Barbados' beauty and charm by packing your luggage, and embracing the laid-back island ambiance. Whether it's your first time or a repeat journey, the island will undoubtedly create an impact and compel you to return.

- ***Tips for an Unforgettable Trip***

This vital travel advice can help you have a genuinely amazing vacation in Barbados:

1. Plan Ahead: To make the most of your stay in Barbados, research and plan your schedule. Make a flexible plan that allows for spontaneity and take into account the sights, activities, and events you want to experience.

2. Best Time to Visit: The best time to go is between December and April because of the beautiful weather in Barbados, which has a tropical environment. However, traveling in the off-peak months of May through June and

November may result in lower costs and less congestion.

3. Packing Essentials: Bring light, comfortable clothes for tropical climates. Important items like sunscreen, hats, and bug repellant shouldn't be overlooked. Pack proper footwear and swimsuits if you want to explore nature paths or engage in water sports.

4. Stay Hydrated: Drink Plenty of Water Barbados may be hot and muggy, so drinking plenty of water is essential. Bring a reusable water bottle with you, and stay hydrated, particularly if you're spending time outside.

5. Stay Connected: Ask your cell service provider about alternatives for international roaming, or think about getting a local SIM card for your phone. Most places in Barbados provide dependable internet access, making it simple for you to remain connected and move across the island.

6. Stay Safe: It's crucial to follow basic safety measures while visiting any new place. Avoid being alone at night, watch your possessions, and use caution while swimming in uncharted waters. To guarantee a secure and comfortable journey, abide by regional laws and traditions.

7. Embrace the Local Culture: Take the time to learn about the regional customs and traditions since Barbados has a rich cultural legacy. Salute someone by saying "Good morning," "Good afternoon," or "Good evening." Respect local customs, clothing requirements, and religious places.

8. Try Local Cuisine: Indulge in Barbados' sensations by sampling the island's food. Try classic foods like cou-cou, flying fish, and macaroni pie. Be sure to sample the renowned Bajan rum, which is an essential component of the island's culture.

9. Interact with the Locals: Barbadians are renowned for their kindness and warmth. Engage in conversation with the locals, seek out their advice, and discover more about their way of life. Participating in local activities may improve your trip and help you make lasting memories.

10. Enjoy the Beaches: Barbados is home to some of the Caribbean's most stunning beaches. Spend some time unwinding, unwinding, and enjoying the sun on the lovely beaches. Be aware of beach safety, heed any warnings that may be posted, and respect the maritime environment.

11. Capture Memories: Barbados is a really beautiful place, so don't forget to pack a camera or smartphone to record the spectacular vistas, lively festivals, and special moments of your stay.

12. Be Flexible and Open-minded: Be adaptable and open-minded, and embrace the laid-back island atmosphere by being receptive to new experiences and interactions. The greatest unforgettable experiences sometimes occur when you least expect them.

You'll be well-equipped to enjoy an amazing vacation to Barbados if you abide by this travel advice. Create lifelong memories while embracing the island's warmth, beauty, and culture.

Printed in Great Britain
by Amazon